YOU SHALL Overcome

A JOURNEY THROUGH ADVERSITY TO VICTORY

MAXINE HENRY

Largo, MD

Copyright © 2024 Maxine Henry

All rights reserved under the international copyright law. No part of this book may be reproduced or transmitted in any form or by any means, electronic or mechanical, including photocopying, recording, or by any information storage and retrieval system, without the express, written permission of the publisher or the author. The exception is reviewers, who may quote brief passages in a review.

Christian Living Books, Inc.
We bring your dreams to fruition.
ChristianLivingBooks.com

ISBN 9781562296476

Unless otherwise indicated, all Scripture quotations are from the King James Version of the Bible. Scripture quotations marked (AMP) are taken from the Amplified Bible®, Copyright © 1954, 1958, 1962, 1964, 1965, 1987, by The Lockman Foundation. Scripture quotations marked GNT are from the Good News Translation in Today's English Version- Second Edition Copyright © 1992 by American Bible Society. Scripture quotations marked (MSG) are taken from THE MESSAGE, Copyright © by Eugene H. Peterson 1993, 1994, 1995, 1996, 2000, 2001, 2002. Used by permission of NavPress Publishing Group. Scripture quotations marked (NLT) are taken from the New Living Translation, Copyright © 1996, 2004, 2007 by Tyndale House Foundation. All right reserved worldwide

Endorsements

When we confront the truth, we embark on a transformative journey that is arduous but ultimately liberating. The grace of God guides us towards a life unshackled by past injustices. May we find wisdom to discern which stories to share as our personal journey unfolds.

Maxine Henry vulnerably recounts her story of struggle and ultimate victory. May it inspire you to embark on a journey of healing and self-discovery and guide you toward truth and inner peace. Grant yourself the gift of graced perspective, and let faith be your lens as you journey through this author's experiences.

Henry's powerful words resonate deeply: 'When someone is violated, they are not just broken, they are shattered.' Readers worldwide who feel broken will find hope in these pages, and stolen joy will be restored. This book will inspire you to cherish life's beauty and embrace the gift of healing.

Congratulations, Maxine Henry, for sharing your courageous story! May your work be a resolution that pain can be acknowledged and overcome. May it inspire others to find their voice, rise above suffering, and bring hope and healing to those who need it. We are overwhelmed by the impact of our testimony, and in our human frailty, we yield ourselves to be used mightily for God's glory.

–Vicki L Kemp
Best Selling Author

Trauma can be crippling and life-altering. It leaves deep emotional wounds that can fester into shame, fear, rage, and insecurities, distorting self-perception and hindering healing. Maxine Henry shares her journey of reclaiming identity and self-love as she faced trauma with great determination to overcome. You too can fight for your healing. Let the hurt of healing be your path to wholeness. Just like Maxine Henry, courage, strength, resilience, and healing can be your portion. You can overcome by being honest with yourself and getting the help and support you need!

–Dr. Niesha Davis-Massey, ThD, LCSW, Trauma Therapist
Author of *Your Story Does Not Define You*

This book beautifully presents God as the saving grace for all things. Maxine's story is familiar to many young girls—a tale of trauma and overcoming adversity. It illustrates how setting your eyes on the Lord can help you overcome anything the enemy meant for harm.

–Odessa (Dess) Perkins, MBA, MS Ed.
Counseling w/PPS Credential, Masters in Educational Specialist
Founder & CEO, emPOWERment Dess Perkins Foundation

Evangelist Maxine Henry shares how a deep relationship with God is essential in helping us understand that while we will face challenges, we must not allow them to paralyze us. Instead, we should gain strength and courage to overcome these obstacles, empowering us to inspire and ignite courage in others to rise above their pain. By doing so, we will reach the heights God has designed for us to attain.

–Jerry E. Scott
Former Superintendent, Lost Hills Union School District

Empowering survivors of domestic violence and molestation to reclaim their voice and soul is at the heart of my advocacy. Congratulations to Maxine Henry for sharing her courageous story and inspiring others with her journey from trauma to triumph. Her resilience testifies to the transformative power of healing and support. May her book encourage compassionate and informed conversations about the struggles others face. By speaking out, we can build a safer, more supportive community for all. I have witnessed abuse countless times. The courage of victims turned survivors fuels my passion for empowering marginalized voices, sparking a movement that can bring liberation and healing to individuals and communities worldwide.

–Leisa Wynn-Johnson, Abuse Survivor and Advocate
Founder & CEO, No Hands Lifted
Author of First Ladies, Can We Talk?

"We must recognize the weight of our voice in other people's life."
                                                    –Maxine Henry

Dedication

To those who have endured the silent struggles and heavy burdens of abuse, mistreatment, rejection, rape, molestation, abandonment, and the like. Those who wrestle with hatred, resentment, anger, vengeance, bitterness, frustration, and unforgiveness. To those whose upbringing was unstable at best, who may have found themselves in foster care or even homeless.

This book is dedicated to you—the survivors, healers, warriors, and overcomers. Your strength in the face of unimaginable pain inspires us all. May the words within these pages offer you solace, understanding, and a path toward liberation.

To those who have walked this path and continue to seek healing, may you find the courage to embrace your journey with compassion and hope. And to those who support and stand beside the survivors, your love and empathy are the beacons that guide them through the darkness.

In honor of your resilience and with deepest respect.

Contents

Preface	xi
Introduction	xiii
Chapter 1 – My Childhood	1
Chapter 2 – I Trusted You	15
Chapter 3 – What in the World Just Happened?	27
Chapter 4 – Violated	41
Chapter 5 – It Was Bigger Than That	55
Chapter 6 – I Am Not What Happened to Me	65
Chapter 7 – Continue to Fight	75
Chapter 8 – You. Shall. Overcome!	85
Chapter 9 – The Power of Forgiveness	95
Chapter 10 – Emerging Victorious	103
Conclusion	109
Appendix A - Kingdom Toolbox	111
Appendix B - Your Glow-Up Guide	117
Appendix C - Resources	119
Acknowledgments	123
About the Author	129

Preface

As I reflect on my journey, I'm compelled to reach back through time and speak to the little girl I once was. If I could wrap my arms around her and whisper words of encouragement, this is what I would say:

Dear Little Max,

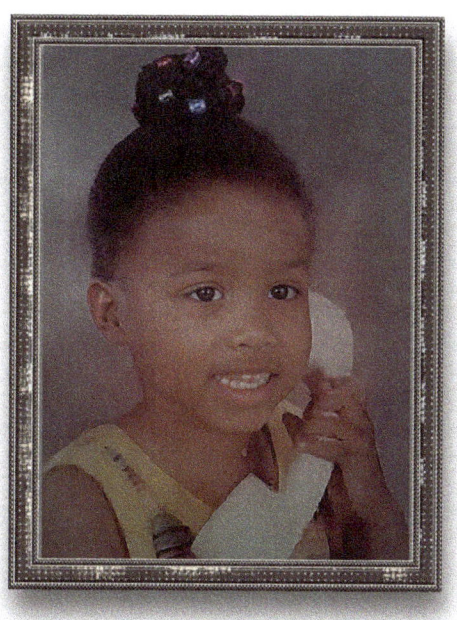

You are such a beautiful girl. Intelligent. Brilliant. A nation shifter. You are filled with wisdom. You are strong. You are resilient. You are priceless. You are important. You are valuable. You are loved. You can do anything you put your mind to. You will not fail. You are an overcomer. You matter.

Your smile lights up rooms. Your skin color is perfect. Your hair texture is perfect. The color of your eyes is perfect. Your nose is perfect. Your lips are the perfect size and shape. Yes, you are perfect and beautiful just the way you are.

You are God's favorite daughter. You are His masterpiece, and He made you exactly how He envisioned you in His mind. He handcrafted you with not one mistake made. Don't ever forget that. God had so much in mind for you when He created you. So many people He destined you to meet. So many places He destined you to go. So many lives He destined you to impact. So, you must stay focused.

Our voice is powerful so think very carefully about what you say to yourself and about yourself. Some days will be tougher than others, but it's ok. When the tough days come and you need encouragement, remember what you have read in this letter. You will make it through them all. If you find that you need someone talk to and no one is around, talk to God. He will always listen. He will always be there. He will always love you. He will always accept you, and you can always trust Him.

One day, you will be grown with a husband and children of your own. Share this letter with them. I have a feeling they might need to hear these words too. Finally, love you. Cherish you. Value you. Choose you. You are worth it. Now, go conquer the world! Your future is waiting for you!

With all my love,

Maxine

Introduction

My obedience to God led me to write what you will read in the pages of this book. While writing, I smiled and laughed; at other times, I cried and pressed through some of my darkest memories. I had to relive the events of my past, allowing myself to feel and articulate every emotion that I did not have language for when I was so young. It was by no means an easy feat. But it was, however, necessary. It was necessary because some little girl or boy's voice has been taken away. I am their voice. It was necessary because some little girls or boys don't quite understand how to convey what they have experienced or are experiencing. I have conveyed for them. It was necessary because those little girls and boys grow up to be young women and men who have suffered for years in silence, not realizing how much their past experiences affected their lives. I have written this book to aid in their understanding.

As you embark on this journey with me, I invite you to consider the letter in the Preface. Those words, penned by my older self to the little girl I once was, encapsulate the essence of what I've learned through my struggles and triumphs. They represent the voice I wish I had heard in my darkest moments—a voice of unconditional love, unwavering support, and profound hope. This letter serves as a beacon, not just for my younger self but for anyone who has ever felt lost, undervalued, or broken. It's a testament to the transformative power of self-love and faith, reminding us that no matter what we've been through, we are inherently valuable and capable of overcoming. As we delve into my story, I encourage you to hold onto the spirit of that letter, for it is the foundation upon which this entire narrative of healing and empowerment is built.

This book was necessary to encourage someone that they too can press through dark memories and moments and come out on the other side victorious. I am that encouragement. This book was necessary to shed light on the darkness that lay tucked away in the tiniest corner of the hearts of many. By the grace of God, I am that light. This book was necessary to encourage some little girl or boy trapped in a young woman or man to know that speaking out about their experiences is okay and that their story is needed. I am their example.

So, when led by God, share with another young girl, boy, man, or

woman about how God brought you through. Right now, some little girls and boys are experiencing the unthinkable. Some little girls and boys are suffering in silence, intimidated and terrified of the one who is and has been violating them. Right now, some little girls and boys are ashamed and embarrassed about what happened, and our story just might provide the strength they need to say something.

It's time to break the silence and shine a light on the widespread issue of sexual abuse. While it's true that this problem affects people all over the world, there is still reason to hope for healing and growth. We can create a culture of support and empowerment by engaging in open and honest conversations. Let's work together to build a brighter future for all.

My dream is to be a catalyst for change, helping those who have been marginalized and oppressed to find their voice and assert their dignity. By speaking out and sharing my experiences, I can help create a world where everyone can thrive and feel valued. Or might I say I'm trying?

My motivation is the fire that fuels my triumph. My passion for supporting those who have faced similar challenges ignites my purpose. The power to overcome any obstacle lies within us all. We must claim our freedom from the clutches of our adversaries.

As you journey through my story, may you discover the strength and courage to overcome any challenge. Let it inspire you to be a beacon of hope and support for those who have been wronged and to ignite a fire of positivity and change in the world around you. Speaking out, no matter how difficult, allows us to break free from the shackles of pain. As we share our experiences, we empower each other to confront the hurts that bind us and uncover the strength within ourselves.

Forty years later, I am able to share what has followed me for so long. For forty years, I carried the condemnation, shame, and guilt of what happened. For forty years, I wore the painful feeling of humiliation and embarrassment, believing that everyone knew my secret. Because of shame, I hid. But one day, I had an encounter with the God of all grace! He assured me that there was, therefore, now no condemnation to those who are in Christ Jesus (Romans 8:1). He said in Isaiah 54:4 not to feel humiliated or ashamed, for you will not be disgraced. For you will forget the shame of your youth. It's as if He inspired these words just for me!

By His Word, I have been restored and made new. This same word applies to you, too. It doesn't matter how long you have been holding in feelings of shame, guilt, and condemnation for what you experienced; you can overcome too. Some young girl or boy is stuck in the same space that God freed me from. Although the enemy meant it for evil, God turned it around for His glory and my good. You may never decide to share your story in a book, in public conversations, or on platforms. But be free. Be free in your mind and your heart. Break free and allow God to be glorified in and through you.

Let's ignite a revolution of courage, compassion, and growth. People, family, friends, community, church, and world… let us merge in empowering the voices of victimized children. May we all speak up loud and clear, even if it's just a glimpse of hope. If you have spoken, then speak again even louder.

INTRODUCTION

I reflect on the days of my life when you could not have told me I would experience such a thing. The tears that I cried, I realize now is the fuel for this book that another young girl or boy or woman or man will read and heal. My motive is clear, my voice is strong, and my story will make a meaningful impact, inspiring change for the better.

Sexual assault is a devastating trauma that can leave deep scars, impacting every facet of life. For those who have faced such a harrowing experience, the path to recovery may seem insurmountable, and the shadows of despair may feel overwhelming. Yet, within these pages, you will find a beacon of hope and a path to healing grounded in the unwavering strength of faith.

The journey to overcoming such a profound violation begins with acknowledging that, while the struggle is real, the power to overcome it lies within reach. In the Bible, we find not only solace but also empowering promises that remind us of our resilience and potential for recovery. The book of Revelation makes it clear.

> They triumphed over him by the blood of the Lamb
> and by the word of their testimony. (Revelation 12:11)

This powerful verse speaks to the strength that comes from faith and personal testimony, not just any testimony, but the testimony of Jesus Christ. From a biblical perspective, the testimony of Jesus Christ often refers to the message and witness of Jesus as recorded in the New Testament. This includes His teachings, His life, His death, and His resurrection. For example, Revelation 19:10 states, "For the testimony of Jesus is the spirit of prophecy." This suggests that the message of Jesus is foundational to understanding prophetic revelations and the broader message of the Bible.

For us as believers, the testimony of Jesus Christ is also about our personal experiences and transformations through our faith in Him. Our testimony often includes stories of how Jesus has impacted our lives, providing hope, healing, and direction. It reminds us that we are not defined by our suffering but by our ability to rise above it, drawing strength from our faith and sharing our stories as a testament to our endurance. Additionally, the testimony of Jesus Christ includes the accounts of His life and work as recorded by the New Testament writers and early Christian witnesses. These accounts form the basis of Christian belief and doctrine. We overcome the enemy by the words of our testimony about what Christ has done in and through our lives.

You might ask the question, what is endurance? How can you even measure endurance? Endurance primarily refers to the ability to remain steadfast in faith and commitment to God despite difficulties, temptations, or suffering. It involves holding firm to one's beliefs and trust in God even when faced with challenges. Endurance is not measured by specific metrics but rather by personal experience and the ability to maintain faith and integrity over time. Endurance is also measured by its outcomes: how it leads to spiritual growth, strengthens character, and enhances one's witness to others.

The ultimate measure is how well a person remains faithful and hopeful in the face of trials. Biblical endurance is about enduring faithfulness and patience through life's challenges, reflecting an unwavering trust in God and an understanding that trials lead to spiritual maturity and growth. It's not measured by specific standards but by the transformative effects it has on an individual's character and spiritual journey. In short, endurance is when you continue to stand and be strong over the very thing that could have stopped you. Think about it!

Jesus Himself offers us a profound promise of victory over adversity. He says:

> In this world you will have trouble. But take heart!
> I have overcome the world. (John 16:33)

This assurance that Christ has overcome all obstacles provides us with a model of triumph and a source of hope, affirming that we can overcome our struggles with His strength.

The Apostle Paul, in his letter to the Romans, encourages us with the words, "In all these things we are more than conquerors through him who loved us" (Romans 8:37). This verse emphasizes that through Christ's love, we are empowered to be more than just survivors; we are overcomers, equipped to face and transcend our deepest challenges. Listen, even when it's hard, painful, frustrating, and you are angry… keep fighting until you can begin to feel the emotions lifting towards a positive change. It is tough when you have been harmed in any manner. Let us be honest and transparent. It is tough.

As we embark on this journey of healing, let us hold fast to the belief that we are capable of overcoming our pain and disappointments. Philippians 4:13 reinforces this truth: "I can do all this through Christ who gives me strength." This promise reminds us that with faith, perseverance, and the strength provided by God, we can indeed overcome the trials that confront us.

In this book, you will discover guidance, inspiration, and a story or two about some things I faced and how I emerged as an overcomer by the grace and mercy of God. May you find renewed strength and hope through my shared experiences and the wisdom of Scripture.

Together, let us embrace the journey of healing and rise above our pain, fortified by faith and the unshakable assurance that with the help of the Lord, we can overcome. Welcome to a path of recovery, transformation, and divine strength. I pray that this book will cause you to look at someone else's life and realize that the world is full of adversity and problems; however, we can all help to be a source of healing, advocacy, and encouragement. I am humbled to allow the world to sit on the front row of my life through this book and envision what little girls have experienced. May it empower you to also be a voice for the voiceless. There is hope, victory, and a great future ahead. I speak life. I speak healing and wholeness.

Chapter 1
MY CHILDHOOD

Dark–devoid or partially devoid of light, not receiving, reflecting, transmitting, or radiating light.

All I see is darkness. Dark days. Dark nights. A dark past. A dark present. A dark future. No matter which way I turn, I am met with darkness. I'm suffocating. I can't breathe. Hello? Is anybody there? Can somebody help me? How will I ever make it out of this? How will I ever get past this place? Will I ever make it out?

You may be wondering what place I'm talking about. This place is a two-block-long street leading to nowhere other than destruction, jail, or death. The two-block long street between California Avenue and Fourth Street, Union Avenue. Union Ave was home to pimps and prostitutes, drug abusers and dope dealers, the runaways, transients, the rejected, the outcast, and for some, their children too. These types were normal to me. They were familiar to me. They were once me. This is where I lived. This is where I learned to survive the streets and become street savvy. The Block, although open-ended on either side, was a dead end. This was home.

At least, as I look back, this is what the enemy wanted me to believe. The enemy wanted me to believe that things don't get any better than this. The enemy wanted me to believe that this was all life had to offer. The enemy wanted me to believe that this was where I would die.

As a young girl, I learned how to survive. I learned early in my life that who I was had to be tucked away tightly so I wouldn't be taken advantage of again. I learned that I could not be the real me. So, I learned how to be someone else.

I had become skilled in hiding my authentic self. I had become masterful at keeping my heart so guarded. I had become a specialist at not allowing the tenderness of my heart to be exposed. I created a version of myself that became my reality, and somewhere in the process of surviving, I lost control of who I had become.

Behind Bars

Have you had to alter who you were to protect your REAL self? Or not show your authentic self out of fear of being hurt or taken advantage of? What barriers have you put in place to keep yourself guarded? What walls have you erected? My cover-up was not having regard for my life or the lives of others. On one hand, I was a protector, yet on the other hand, I had no regard for life. Well, that's what I wanted people to believe. The alteration of who we are, the barriers, the walls, and the lack of regard for life are all defense mechanisms,

specifically reaction formation. According to *Psychology Today*, reaction formation is defined as "Behaving or expressing the opposite of one's true feelings"[1]

I dreaded being taken advantage of again, so I did exactly the opposite of what I truly felt. In my mind, I was protecting myself. In my mind, I was in control. In my mind, I had it all figured out. What I didn't realize was that building barriers and walls to keep people out kept me in. Out of fear of being mistreated, I created a cage for the real me, locking me in while trying to keep others out. This is one of many deceptions of the enemy!

I'm reminded of a portion of truth found in the Bible that states, "The thief comes only to steal and kill and destroy." (John 10:10 AMP). Did you read that? Let me explain what was just stated in this text. The enemy, Satan, the devil, doesn't show up unless it's to steal something from us, kill us, or perhaps kill something in us, or destroy us! That is his entire agenda. He's not showing up for any other reason! And because I didn't know any better, I had no idea that this reaction formation was part of the subtle plan of the enemy to destroy my future.

But… The Father had a plan for my life! In the same way He had a plan for my life, He has a plan for you too! I wasn't aware then, but the second half of John 10:10 says, "I [Jesus] came that they may have life, and have

> **BUT… THE FATHER HAD A PLAN FOR MY LIFE!**

it in abundance [to the full, till it overflows]" (John 10:10 AMP). It's The Father's desire for us to live a life overflowing and not a life of mediocrity.

---

[1] https://www.psychologytoday.com/us/basics/defense-mechanisms

Even though I had created this revised version of myself, deep down within, I believed there was a way out, even though I didn't know The Father's desire for my life. I believed education would be the vehicle, so I decided to let school drive. I believed the only way I would make it off the block was by staying in school and getting an education. I believed there had to be more than where I was, and the only way I would find out about that "more" was to learn about it. So, I did.

One of my initial sources of learning about "more" was *The Cosby Show*. Do you remember *The Cosby Show*? That was my show! The Huxtables: an upper-middle-class black family. Cliff Huxtable, the father, was an OBGYN, while Claire Huxtable was a lawyer. Together, they had five children: four girls, Sondra, Denise, Vanessa, and Rudy, and one boy, Theo. I identified most with Rudy, the youngest. I was the youngest in my family, too. We were around the same age.

Rudy had the life I often dreamt about. She lived in a beautiful two-story home in an upper-middle-class neighborhood in Brooklyn, NY. Both of her parents worked great jobs and always showed how much they loved her. She always laughed and joked with her sisters and brother. At dinner time, they all ate around the table, discussed the events of their day, and planned things to do.

Soul Food

The dinner table represents family time, communion, and fellowship. Although discussions take place in other parts of the home, the dinner table is where the whole family gathers and talks as a family unit and spends quality time with one another. The dinner table was the one area of the home where some of the most essential knowledge was passed down, and love was expressed through food.

I arrived at my initial conclusion about what a loving family looked like by how The Huxtables gathered and talked around the dinner table, among other things. They all seemed so happy. Rudy seemed to not have a care in the world. Sometimes, when I watched the show, I would envision myself in Rudy's place. I imagined Cliff and Claire being my parents and Rudy's siblings my siblings. *The Cosby Show* was my getaway.

This family was my dream. I even decided I wanted to be an OB/GYN, just like my dream dad, Dr. Huxtable. I wanted to deliver babies just like him. My dream dad was amazing! He brought new life into the world every day! I wanted to do that, too. Even though I kept my real feelings for life hidden, I wanted to bring life into the world. Regardless of whether Cliff and Claire worked together, they always did things as a family and for the family.

In "Happy Anniversary" (Season 2, Episode 3), the family planned to serenade Cliff's parents for their 49th wedding anniversary. This was my absolute favorite episode! The grandparents were seated next to each other in the living room at Rudy's house, waiting for the entertainment to begin. Cliff cuts on the record player, and an infamous blues song, "(Night Time Is) The Right Time" by the late Ray Charles, begins to play. Theo walks downstairs, in tune with the tempo of the music. Claire and the girls are the backup dancers and singers. When the beat drops, Theo begins to lip-sync:

> You know the night time, darling (night and day)
>
> Is the right time (night and day)
>
> To be (night and day)
>
> With the one you love, now (night and day)
>
> Say now, oh baby (night and day)

> When I come home baby, now (night and day)
> I wanna be with the one I love, now (night and day)
> You know what I'm thinking of (night and day)
> I know the night time (night and day, oh)
> Whoa, is the right time (night and day, oh)
> To be with the one you love, now (night and day)
> I said to be with the one you love (night and day)
> Whoah! sing your song, Margie"

Rudy comes in with:

> Baby (night and day)
> Baby (night and day)
> Baby (night and day)
> Oh, baby (night and day)
> Do I love you? (night and day)
> No one above you (night and day)
> Hold me tight (night and day)
> And make everything all right (night and day)
> Because the night time (night and day)
> Oh, is the right time (night and day)
> To be with the one you love now (night and day)
> Oh yeah (night and day)"

Dad Huxtable sings:

> I said baby (night and day)
> Baby (night and day)

Baby (night and day)

Whoah! baby now (night and day)

Oh come on baby (night and day)

You know I want you by my side (night and day)

I want you to keep (night and day)

Oh keep me satisfied (night and day)

I know the night time (night and day)

Everyday is the right time (night and day)

Yeah to be with the one you love now (night and day)

Well you know it's all right"[2]

I would laugh so hard whenever I saw this part of the episode. Rudy was so cute. What made it so funny when Rudy was singing was that she was so small compared to the others, and one of her front teeth was missing. She was the smallest performing but lip-synched the biggest part of the song!

I would get into character and reenact this episode repeatedly, laughing hysterically at myself each time. The grandparents seemed to enjoy and appreciate the kid's rendition of the song. The family had put some thought into this to make Grandma and Grandpa's anniversary one to remember. If you haven't seen this part of that episode, you should go watch it. It's on YouTube.

---

[2] https://www.musixmatch.com/lyrics/Ray-Charles/Night-Time-Is-the-Right-Time. Songwriters: Lew Herman Herman / Lubinsky. The Right Time lyrics © Screen Gems EMI Music Inc., Songs of Universal Inc., Arc Music Corp, Prestige Music Co Inc.

Narrow Horizons

Dreadfully, that wasn't my reality, though. My reality was pimps, prostitutes, drug users, and drug dealers. That was it. Those were my options. That's all I had to choose from. I had to choose, so I chose the latter. With such great options (note the extreme sarcasm here), you may be wondering how I came to the conclusion I did. It's simple. Remember I told you that I kept who I was tucked away tight? Well, who I was wouldn't allow me to participate in certain things. For instance, I couldn't be a pimp because they exploited the young girls. They abused them mentally, physically, emotionally, and financially!

> **MY REALITY WAS PIMPS, PROSTITUTES, DRUG USERS, AND DRUG DEALERS.**

The real me didn't and still doesn't like to see people taken advantage of, mistreated, or done wrong. I'm immediately triggered. I'm a fixer, and pimps didn't fix things; they broke things. They broke the girl's will. They broke her spirits. They broke her heart. They broke her life. So, pimping wouldn't work for me.

I couldn't be a prostitute. Although I didn't think too much of myself, I believed myself to be more valuable and precious than to settle for selling myself for a couple of dollars. I didn't have much, but I refused to be the person to go work hard for something and sell my body for a little of nothing just to give it to some guy who wanted to look like more than what he was. I didn't believe there was enough money a trick could pay me to lay down with him. Something in me knew I was worth more than that. I couldn't be a prostitute.

Being a crackhead was absolutely out of the question! I grew up around them. I saw what the drugs did to them. I saw how they lost everything, including themselves, just to get high for a few minutes. I saw how the women and men alike prostituted themselves just to support their habit. I was even in the hotel room with them while they turned tricks and witnessed how they demeaned and degraded themselves just for a fix. Drug user? Nah. I was smarter than that. I had a line I refused to cross.

The Logical Choice

The only logical thing to do was to be the dealer. Not because I wanted to get rich. Not because I wanted to have a lot of things. But because the dope dealer always had money to eat. He always had money to pay for a place to sleep. He always had money to buy clothes to wear. So that's what I did.

I hustled to have money to eat, pay for a hotel room for the night, and buy something to wear to school. I went to school in the daytime and hustled at night. I was sure to do all my work while at school, so I didn't have to bring the work home. At school, I could get help if needed. The people back home, on the block, couldn't help me.

I bought clothes every day to wear to school the next day and made sure I had a place to sleep and something to eat. If I looked presentable, I wouldn't draw attention to myself and my current situation; I would fly under the radar, just like I did. I was a thinker, though, at times, I failed to think as I should have.

Hustling didn't come without risk, though. I had to constantly look over my shoulder, watching not only for the police but also for the robber. There seemed to always be someone looking for an easy come-up, hiding around corners and lurking in the shadows, looking to catch someone slipping. So, I invested in some protection, a security guard, if you will. My best friend at the time. PEACE. I purchased a little black .380. Peace was just small enough for my hand and my pocket. As long as I had Peace, I had peace. After all, home was anything but peaceful.

There Has to Be More

The block was riddled with fights, stabbings, shootings, murders, robberies, kidnappings, rapes, etc. You name it, home had it. Home had a lot of things, but it didn't have anything like "I love you, daughter." There was no "I'm proud of you." There was no "You're doing a great job." At home, there was no love. I often thought, "There has to be more to life than this." At this time in my life, I knew nothing about Christ, but somehow, I knew there was more to life than the block and I was determined to find out what that "more" was.

I arrived in Bakersfield from Los Angeles in February of 1984 at the tender age of six. It was a complete culture shock! Although I was as young as I was, I noticed a BIG difference between city life and country life. Everything was different. Before moving to Bakersfield, I lived in the part of Los Angeles known as "The Jungle,"—3905 Stevely Avenue, Apt 5, to be exact.

Our apartment was upstairs. We had neighbors on either side. I had a friend named Bertha. Bertha was nice. She was always

nice to me. She was darker skinned with long, thick, pretty hair. She was teased a lot by the other kids in the apartments because she had a keloid on her ear. I liked her, though. Her imperfections didn't matter to me. Aside from being one of the younger, smaller kids in the complex, I didn't like the way Bertha was teased, but I was too little to do anything about it. This feeling would never leave me as I grew older.

There was something very protective about me. I didn't like to see people hurt, teased, and mistreated. Even now, in my adult life, I still don't like to see people taken advantage of and wronged. Now, I'm big enough to say something, to speak out against it. It took a while, but I have finally found my voice, and I intend to use it to speak up and out against the maltreatment of others.

I can remember being caught between my love for my dad and my love for my mom. Mom was a sweet, hard-working woman who sometimes worked two jobs to do her part in the household. Her name is Rovetta. Different, huh? Her friends called her "Rita." Mom worked at Queen of Angels Hospital as a medical biller by day and as an answering service representative in the evenings.

The Princess and the Superhero

I don't remember where Dad worked. Dad's name is Harold. One night, I remember Mom having cooked black-eyed peas. I was sitting in Mom's lap next to Dad when he bit into a rock. Mom must have missed it during the cleaning process before cooking and serving Dad his plate. Dad got so upset! He began yelling and cursing at Mom and slapped her across the face while I was sitting on her lap! Her glasses flew across the room, and she began to weep. I hated seeing Dad and Mom fight. I hated seeing her crying. I hated seeing him upset. I didn't like him hitting Mom, but I didn't like Mom making Dad mad. I was torn between the two.

Dad never hit me. He never let Mom hit me, either. He was my protector. Even though he and Mom would fight, I always felt safe with him. He never let anyone hurt me. He never yelled at me. He never cursed at me. He was my safe place. We always had fun. He would let me sit on his lap and drive around the parking lot. Mom didn't know, though, because she would be mad. The car was so huge! It seemed to be a mile long to me… lol. A mustard colored 1976 Cutlass Supreme. I could barely see over the steering wheel even while sitting on Dad's lap. I was so little, and the steering wheel seemed so massive! I remember having to use both hands just to turn! Those were fun times.

> **I HATED SEEING DAD AND MOM FIGHT.**

One night, Mom and Dad had friends over—Linda and Pete. The music was blaring, "Just because you're not for real, why do you desire to hurt me, girl? Just because you're not for real, why do you want to hurt me, girl?"[3] They loved listening to loud music and hanging out with Linda and Pete. Sometimes, it was Kool & The Gang; other times, it was The Whispers, Earth Wind & Fire, Teena Marie, Teddy Pendergrass, Marvin Gaye, or Peaches & Herb. I guess this is where I developed a love for music. There was always music playing. If Mom and Dad were fighting, music was playing. If they were entertaining company, music was playing. When Mom was cleaning, there was music playing. Mom and Dad loved music.

---

3   genius.com/The-gap-band-burn-rubber-on-me-why-you-wanna-hurt-me-lyrics.

One night, they were dancing and laughing. Mom and Dad were in a great mood and getting along. Everyone seemed to be enjoying themselves when suddenly, I tripped and fell, busting my eye open on the glass coffee table. Everything in the apartment was glass and brass back then; blame it on the 1970s and early 1980s. Blood was everywhere, and I was crying uncontrollably. As I'm crying, Mom is panicking.

Mom is probably hemophobic. People suffering from hemophobia have a fear of blood. They have an extreme or irrational dread of the sight of blood, even to the point of refusing to go to the doctor if they know blood will be drawn. They may experience difficulty breathing, sweating, anxiety, or even fainting.[4]

I don't remember Mom passing out, but she definitely panicked. Not Dad, though. Dad picked me up, began wiping my face, and calmed me down like only he could. My whole world would be ok if my Dad was there. I was his princess, and he was my superhero. However, that all changed when we left Los Angeles.

> **A Little Girl's Recommendation:** Please pay attention to me. Please look into my eyes and see me. Please observe even the slightest changes in my behavior.

My Prayer for Little Girls

Father, I pray for the protection of little girls. I pray You cover them with the blood of Your Son, Jesus, and keep them from dangers seen and unseen. I pray Your angels stand guard over them and fight for them, especially since they are too small to fight for themselves. I pray their parents realize the

---

[4] https://www.osmosis.org/answers/hemophobia.

importance and significance of both parents in their lives. May little girls everywhere find safety and security in You and Your desire for their lives. May You be enough. May You be the object of their affections and the one their hearts long for. May they come to know and understand that even when no one else is looking out for them, You are. In Jesus' name. Amen.

Chapter 2
I TRUSTED YOU

Trust–the assured reliance on the character, ability, strength, or truth of someone or something; to rely on the truthfulness or accuracy of; belief.[5]

What does trust mean? Often, we choose to trust those who have demonstrated a level of trustworthiness based on our past experiences, cultural biases, upbringing, and expectations. When a person's behaviors line up with our expectations of them, we trust them. When a person believes the way we believe, we trust them. When a person is taught the way we were taught, we tend to trust them. When a person's experiences are the same or similar to ours, we tend to lean more toward them. Why? We trust those with whom we can relate and who have similar opinions, thought processes, and viewpoints on certain issues. For most of us, our trust in others is based more on how we can identify with them. We trust based on our emotions as opposed to character, integrity, morals, ethics, and values.

When we place our trust in someone, it should be based on his or her character. When we decide to trust someone, that trust

---

[5] https://www.merriam-webster.com/dictionary/trust

should be based on truth and not emotions. Emotions change. Emotions fluctuate. Truth, however, is constant. The truth remains the same.

This is my forty-five-year-old self talking, thinking, and rationalizing. My six-year-old self couldn't articulate or understand the concept of trust; therefore, I trusted those who were around me. I trusted those who were relatives of mine. I trusted my family. At such a young age, we will not likely understand the importance and value of trusting the right people. At that age, the mind and heart are pure, and there is a void of understanding of such complexities as trust. It's at the stage where trust is violated before its true meaning is ever understood. At least, this is how it was for me. My experience of trust was shaken.

Before moving to Bakersfield, I was only around a few people, and those few were people I trusted. At that time, I believed neither of these individuals would ever do anything to hurt me. I especially knew that my dad wouldn't allow anyone to hurt me. I trusted my dad. He never did anything to cause me to question whether I could trust him or not. Even when I was bad or disobedient, he wouldn't holler at me or spank me.

When my brother and sister would do things to me, I would run to him and tell him, and they would get in trouble. Dad wouldn't even let my mom discipline me! Time and time again, Dad demonstrated that I could always trust him. As I reflect while writing about my dad, I am truly grateful for the love he showed me. The love was real, and his protection of me as a child made me feel safe. Thank you, Dad.

Daddy Issues

As an adult woman, I now realize that many women have insecurities because there is a void if a father isn't in the home. Also, women have abandonment struggles without the faithful presence of a dad in their lives. It makes a difference. The one who has been abandoned feels like they have been left behind and undesired. They feel discarded and unwanted. They feel inadequate and unworthy. They feel rejected and lonely.

Dad hugged me, kissed my cheeks, loved on me, and affirmed me. In contrast, when I was taken away from Dad, I experienced all the emotions mentioned above. I wasn't just taken away from my dad; I was taken away from his protection, his hugs, kisses, love, and affirmation. Who will hug me now? Who will kiss my cheeks now? Who will show my love now? Who will affirm me now? I was left with a void that I longed to fill.

> **I THOUGHT WE WERE JUST GOING TO VISIT.**

Mothers, a father's presence in the life of a young girl reaches beyond the differences you and he may have with one another. What that young girl loses when her father is removed from her life follows her for the rest of her life. She searches for the love she desires from her father in other men. Unfortunately, this search can land a young girl—who remains trapped inside of a grown woman—on the lap and in the bed of a man who doesn't love her at all.

Everything was so different now. I thought we were just going to visit. I was oblivious to what was happening. What I thought was another visit to Grandma's house turned out to be that Mom decided to move us to Bakersfield. Why didn't she talk to me about this? Why didn't she tell me? Didn't she know I wanted to stay with my dad? So many questions!

I had no idea that my life would never be the same on that day in February of 1984. I had no idea that would be one of the last times I would feel safe, secure, and protected during my childhood. I had no idea I would never again be able to run into the arms of the man who had been my trusted place all my little life. I trusted my mom. I trusted my brother. I trusted my sister. But there was no one I trusted the way I trusted my dad. I was taken away, ripped away, snatched away from the one person I knew I could trust. I was uprooted from what I knew as stability and dropped off smack dab in the middle of chaos and confusion.

The same summer we arrived in Bakersfield, Dad came to visit. I was so ecstatic! It was around July 4th. We had so much fun together. I missed him so much. I remember sitting around the dinner table at Grammie's house eating dinner. I didn't want to eat my sweet peas. The little round green ones. Yuck! Dad didn't make me. He was my superhero.

Right at dusk, we went outside and lit fireworks. We were having so much fun! He even danced over the fireworks as they shot up in the air! I was scared he would get burned but excited at the show he was putting on at the same time. I will never forget that day.

His Back

The next morning, at breakfast, I didn't want to eat my eggs. Dad ate them for me. He always bailed me out. We hung out for a while until it was time for him to leave. I hated that our time together had to end. How I wish he could have stayed.

The day he left is cemented in my memory. As we were saying our goodbyes, my face was soaked with tears. My young mind had no comprehension of why he had to leave and why I wasn't allowed to go with him. All I knew was that I wanted my life with Dad to go back to the way it was before. Us. Together. It's not fair! Wow! Why? Somebody help me! Can anybody see what's happening to me? NO?!

Today, I can still see him walking east, up the street, each step he took cutting deeper, the pain getting stronger and each sob growing louder. When he began walking off, he never said another word. He just walked. Leaving me standing in the middle of the street. Crying. Was he crying too? Was he hurting as much as I was? He never looked back or even glanced over his shoulder. It didn't matter to him how loud I screamed and how hard I cried. It didn't matter. I stood there, bawling my eyes out, wishing he would turn around. Wishing he would come back. He just kept walking.

> **THE MOST POWERFUL IMAGE OF DAD IS OF HIM WALKING AWAY.**

Although I've heard his voice one time since then, that agonizing day was the last time I would ever see him. The most powerful image of him is not the fun times. It's not any of the memories of the times we shared in Los Angeles. It's not the time we spent when he came to visit that one time. It's not him dancing over the fireworks. It's his back. It's the image of that white shirt and blue jeans getting smaller and smaller as he got further and further away with each step. The most powerful image of Dad is of him walking away.

Country

While in Los Angeles, only five of us lived in the home. It was a typical two-parent household; however, when I arrived in Bakersfield, the place of our new home where we would reside was packed! There were no more two-parent households. There was my Grammy, some of her kids, and some of their kids, all in a two-bedroom project. Thirteen or fourteen people were living in that small place. Yes! Seriously. You talk about a humble beginning.

We slept where we could. Sometimes on the floor, sometimes in the bed. One of the cousins still peed in the bed, so no one wanted to sleep with him. There were seven boys and four girls ranging from about fifteen years old to newborn. I was the youngest girl, and the one under me was one year old. The other was a newborn.

Life here was horrible! It was very country, to say the least. "Country" is a term used for a certain way of living. I'm sure some of you are reading this, and you can relate to it. There was no noise from city life. No cars whizzing up and down the street. No hustle and bustle of life in the fast lane. Everything seemed to be in slow motion, and to top it off, the nearest store seemed miles away.

Shadows of Dread

If that wasn't enough, the people here rode horses, y'all… horses!!! While horse riding may fascinate some, I was anything but fascinated by them. I was petrified of them! They seemed so massive compared to my tiny frame. I was about sixty-five pounds and forty-two inches tall. I could still walk underneath a diesel trailer without ducking down. Standing next to an animal so powerful intimidated me so much. In my mind, if given the opportunity, a horse would take me out with just a single kick from one of those chiseled hind legs. But I wouldn't dare get that close. I kept my distance. As of now, I haven't even done so much as stroke a horse's mane, let alone ride one.

Have you ever been afraid of something and had no idea where the fear of that thing stemmed from? Fear can come into our hearts and minds in many ways. Not only was I petrified of horses, but I was also terrified of dogs. *The Merriam-Webster Dictionary* defines fear as an unpleasant, often strong emotion caused by anticipation of danger. Anticipation of danger. Remember how I said if, given the opportunity, the horse would take me out with a single kick? I was anticipating the worst possible outcome.

I had the same feeling about dogs. True story: I left home walking one day and saw a dog almost at the end of the block. Out of fear, I turned around and went all the way around the block just to avoid encountering the dog. It seems ridiculous to me now, but then not so much. I was so gripped by fear. That's what fear does. It grips you. It wraps its arms around you and sinks its claws into you. Fear paralyzes you from going forward and will even cause you to go backward. The Bible assures us:

> For God hath not given us the spirit of fear, but of power, and of love, and of a sound mind.
> (2 Timothy 1:7)

Fear is a spirit. Fear is of the devil. The Father has not called us to be fearful, cowardly, or timid. He has made us powerful, disciplined, and healthy, with a balanced mind. One day, while in prayer, The Father revealed to me when the spirit of fear grabbed hold of me. He reminded me of a movie I watched as a little girl, *Cujo*. This is when fear crept in.

We must be careful of what we are watching and listening to. We can unknowingly expose ourselves to the enemy, open doors for him to creep into, and wreak havoc in our lives. Now, when I feel fear trying to rise in me, I immediately combat it: "God didn't give me the spirit of fear but power, love, and a sound mind. Satan, the Lord rebuke you. I will not fear. The Lord is my light and my salvation. I don't receive you, and I send you back to the sender. In Jesus' Name!"

Sometimes, the fear goes away quickly, and at other times, not as quickly. However, in those moments, I just continue to work my way through it until it does. There has been a time or two when I would just have to

> **FEEL THE FEAR, BUT DO IT ANYWAY.**

go forward with whatever I needed to do, and the fear would leave somewhere in the middle of my doing. If you are battling with fear, I'll share with you what the Lord instructed me to do: "Feel the fear, but do it anyway."

It's a Different World

Back home in L.A., there weren't any horses to be seen anywhere other than the zoo, and not any being used as a mode of transportation. I don't even remember having encountered any dogs then. Back home, my brother, sister, and I would walk to the store and hide in the clothes, eating donuts and drinking juice while trying not to get caught. Back home, we would run up and down the stairs and all around the complex, playing with the neighboring children. Back home, it was different. The weather was different. The smell was different. The food was different. The people were different. Everything was different.

At home, I was able to be a little girl and enjoy doing so. Playing with baby dolls. Playing with dishes. Tea parties with my dolls. Learning how to love and nurture as I was designed to do. Using my imagination to be whoever I wanted to be during my playtime without concern.

I remember one time wanting to be a Geisha Girl. I thought they were so beautiful, but I never knew their purpose or occupation. Their hair was always pretty. Their make-up was flawless. Their dresses were immaculate. They moved with such fluidity and grace. I would dance around my bedroom mimicking the dance moves or walk around imitating how they walked. I would have so much fun! However, one day, the enemy attempted to rob me of my innocence.

This one day changed my life. On this day, my brother's friend was over. He tried to do "things" to me. He tried to do bad, awful, sad, disgusting things! It was not good at all. Of course, being so young, I still didn't imagine the torment or the pain I would feel as days went by. The shame and confusion that I would now suffer. Remember the trust I talked about? Now, I was confused. He was one of the people I trusted. He was like family. I cried out in pain…

"Ouch! Stop! That hurts!"

That was the first time someone I "trusted" tried to take advantage of me. That would be my brother's friend's first and last time, but unfortunately, it wouldn't be the last time for me.

> **A Little Girl's Recommendation:** Please teach me how to trust and who to trust. Please teach me how to pray at an early age. Please teach me the definition of fear.

My Prayer for Little Girls

Father, I pray a special covering over the hearts and minds of little girls. I pray You show them, at a tender age, that they should and can trust You. I pray that just as You have shown Yourself as trustworthy to me, You do the same for them. I pray for their minds and that they remain pure even though they are in the midst of an impure world. I pray they desire to live for You. I pray for their focus. I pray that You be the center of their attention. I pray they have confidence in You. I pray for the gift of faith to manifest in their life. I pray they place their faith in You and have no other gods besides You, the true and living God. In Jesus' name. Amen.

Chapter 3
WHAT IN THE WORLD JUST HAPPENED?

My heart was racing. My head was spinning. My thoughts were disheveled. My emotions were scattered. My eyes filled with tears. My cookie was sore. What in the world just happened?

I was a happy little girl who enjoyed playing outside with the other little girls in the apartments. We were friends. Occasionally, we would fight over dolls and other toys. You know, things little girls bicker over.

Me: "I want to play with the doll with the long hair."

Friend: "You always play with her! It's my turn!"

Little stuff like that. This day was no different than any other day. When I woke up, I was excited! I wasn't quite old enough for school then, so I had nothing to do but get my brother and sister in trouble. Remember, I always got them in trouble. Especially my brother. It was easy, too, because he was the oldest. I would do stuff I knew I wasn't supposed to do and run to Dad for protection, knowing he would keep me safe.

I remember one time I put a Twinkie in the oven and turned it on so my Twinkie would warm up. In my little mind, it made so much sense! I had watched Mom use the oven many times. I knew that the food went in cold and after some time came out hot. So, I tried to do what I had seen Mom do on nanny occasions. I put the Twinkie in the oven. Wrapper and all! No baking sheet. No foil. No pan. Just the Twinkie in the wrapper on the rack. I laugh at the thought of it today. How innocent I was in my thinking. The intention, this time, was not to get my brother in trouble. It just worked out in my favor... lol.

I turned on the oven and enthusiastically waited for my warm snack. I was oblivious to the fact of the wrapper melting. I was oblivious to the smoke the melted plastic would cause. It never crossed my mind that my Twinkie would burn up and the house would almost catch fire! By the time anyone recognized what I had done, it was almost too late. We went from laughing and joking to panicking at the chaos in the kitchen. I was terrified! It wasn't until I saw how upset Dad was that I realized what a bad thing I had done. I could have burned up the kitchen. I could have burned down the apartment. I could have burned down the complex. I could have killed us! Dad was fuming! And Big Brother got in trouble. I escaped punishment, but he didn't. He was the oldest. He was supposed to be looking after me. I slipped away while his back was turned and nearly killed us all. I didn't want Dad to be mad. But! I was happy that he wasn't mad at me and even happier that he was mad at my brother... lol.

Have you ever done something extremely dangerous from a place of innocence that could have gone wrong? Thinking back, I can see how God has protected me from as far back as I can remember! What a mighty God we serve! The protection of God is like no other. He not only shields us from the enemy, but

He shields us from ourselves. The psalmist encourages us with these words:

> But thou, O LORD, art a shield for me; My glory, and the lifter up of mine head. (Psalm 3:3).

I am so glad I can count on the protection of God! Even when I think He should have protected me differently, I have to

> **THIS WAS BAD, BUT IT COULD HAVE BEEN A WHOLE LOT WORSE.**

thank Him that things didn't go how they could have. There are times in our lives when we must admit, "This was bad, but it could have been a whole lot worse." This was one of those times.

All Our Trust

I can remember it so clearly. We were in my brother's bedroom. It was daylight outside. The sun was shining bright. The birds were singing so beautifully. Peering through the second-story window, it was absolutely gorgeous out there! However, on the inside, not so much. The bedroom wasn't the cleanest. The bed was unmade. The sheets and covers were strewn about. The closet was open and in disarray. Posters were hanging halfway off the walls. Dirty clothes were lying around. Smelly socks and shoes littered the floor. Hot wheel tracks. Cars. Magazines. Action figures. Boys' toys all around. It smelled like feet and a sweaty boys' locker room.

Although the floor was cluttered, somehow, my brother's friend found just enough space for me to lay on. Why was I lying on the floor in my brother's room with this boy in there? Why were we in my brother's room alone? Why was there no supervision? Why was this door partially closed? Oh yeah. I trusted him.

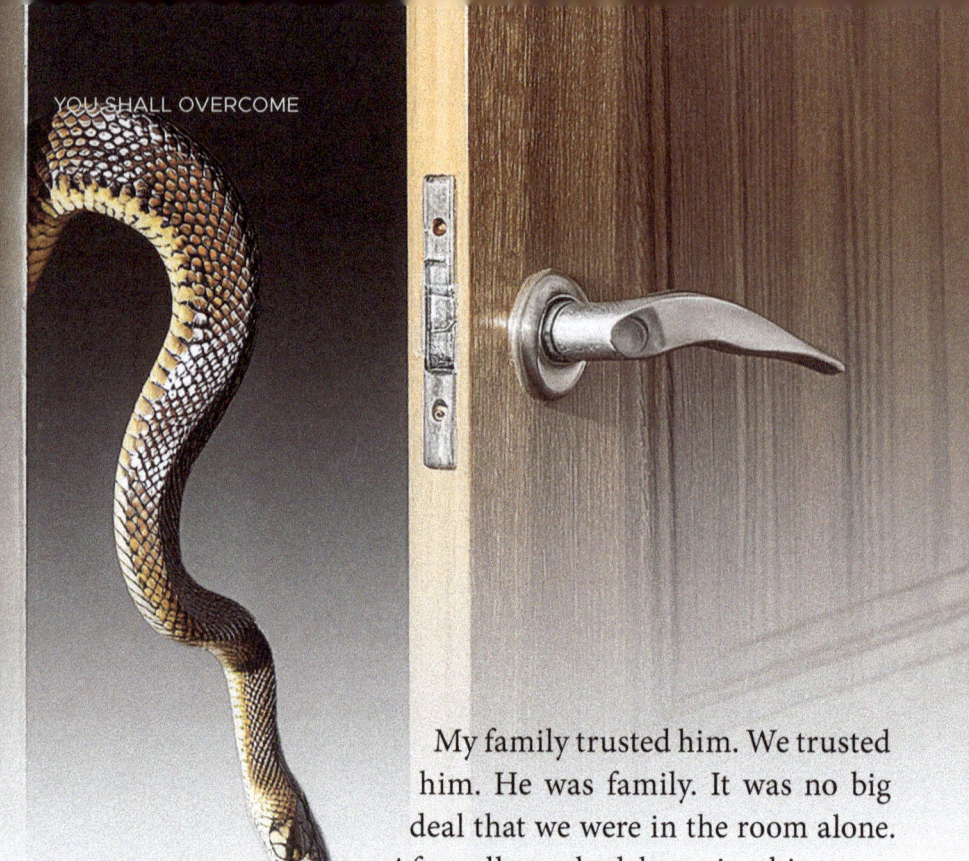

My family trusted him. We trusted him. He was family. It was no big deal that we were in the room alone. After all, we had been in this same room alone plenty of times before. This time was different, though. This time, he saw an opportunity. It was almost as if he waited until he had all of our trust before he made his move.

He was calculated. He was strategic. He was slick. He waited patiently. Day in and day out. Coming over. Playing with my brother and his toys while secretly wanting to "play with me." Eating with us. Gaining our trust. As everyone slowly let down their guard, he became a fixture in the family. I was being hunted. Dad didn't know it. Mom didn't know it. My brother and sister didn't know it. I didn't know it. I was the prey. He was the predator. He had one agenda. STEAL. KILL. DESTROY. When the environment was just right, when the time was right, when our guard was down, he struck. What in the world just happened?

Venom's Kiss

Isn't that just like the enemy? CUNNING. CONNIVING. COWARDLY. Presenting himself as stealthy and powerful but lacking the courage to come head-on. SUCKA! Yeah. That's just what he is. A sucka! The Urban Dictionary describes this as an "old school term for a chump… normally used to remind an adversary that they suck and are known to start mess they can't finish." He seeks an opportunity to take advantage of those he sees as less powerful than him. The one who won't put up a fight. The one who seems timid and easily overpowered. The unsuspecting. The one he can intimidate and blindside, catching them off guard. The Bible warns us about "this kind." The enemy. The adversary. The devil. Satan. The Bible cautions us about the purpose of the enemy. Again, we can reference the Gospel of John:

> The thief's purpose is to steal and kill and destroy.
> (John 10:10a NLT)

He wants to steal your future. He wants to kill your drive, dreams, goals, ambitions, and aspirations! He wants to destroy you. He hates you. He hates me. He hates us! The enemy wanted to steal, kill, and destroy my future before I was even old enough to know what the word future meant.

Looking back, I can see how the enemy snaked his way into our home only to strike while unsuspecting. Today, through the power of the Holy Ghost, I can hear his hiss. Then? I had no clue. I was too young to even comprehend what was taking place. Too young to see his plan unfolding. Too young to recognize the deception. He was so calculated and conniving that he was willing to work through this boy to do it.

I now realize that while trying to destroy me, he planned to simultaneously destroy this young boy's future as well. You see, this was a two-for-one. The plan was to destroy two futures with one event. In another powerful passage of scripture, Peter gives us this vantage point of this same enemy:

> Be alert, be on watch! Your enemy, the Devil, roams around like a roaring lion, looking for someone to devour. (1 Peter 5:8 GNTD)

Then, I knew nothing of being alert and watching. I knew nothing about being on watch. Oh, but I thank God that He has opened my understanding of His Word! Now, I'm alert. Now, I'm sober. Now, I watch. I am no longer that little girl. By the grace of God, I have grown up and matured some in Him!

Predator's Playground

From the beginning, there was an agenda to overpower and overtake the weakest in the house. Me. You see, I was the youngest female, around four years old. Mom was grown, so she was automatically ruled out as prey. My sister was four years older than me but was too big for this boy to overpower. So, that left me. Young. Innocent. Smaller. Weaker. The baby of the bunch. Me. He must have known that I was easy pickings. I'd pose the least challenge. I'd put up the least amount of resistance. I'd be much easier to overpower. Easier to intimidate. Easier to take advantage of. This is the nature of the lion.

> **SO, THAT LEFT ME. YOUNG. INNOCENT. SMALLER. WEAKER.**

I remember in October 2021, a powerhouse preacher, Pastor Shavon Smith, was the guest speaker at the Fireproof Women's

Conference. She preached a message entitled: *There's A Lion In Me*. While this message was meant to encourage and empower women to be bold, resilient, and relentless, I was very much intrigued by her usage of a lion for the analogy. I wanted to take a trip to the zoo to observe the lion's behavior. And that's what I did. In February of 2022, for our 7th wedding anniversary, my husband and I went to San Diego. I told him, "Honey, Pastor Shavon Smith said there's a lion in me, and I want to go see what's in me." His response was "Bet" meaning "Let's go." He's so sweet to me. I love him.

When we arrived at the zoo, the weather was extremely warm. Although it was early February and technically Winter, it was about ninety degrees! But I was on a mission. I had to get to the lion exhibit. We visited several exhibits on the way to the lion's den. We saw animals that we'd never seen before! Baboons, monkeys, vultures, eagles, llamas, camels, elephants, hippos, tortoises, lizards, and many more! I will never forget stopping by Reptile Mesa and seeing the differently colored exotic reptiles. God has created some amazing animals! What a wonderful God we serve.

Invisible Chains

I remember getting to the tanks where the snakes were. I stood in front of the tank, looking closely for what was in the tank. I couldn't see it. Where was it? I looked and looked and looked. Finally, there it was, well hidden and camouflaged by the wildlife in the tank. Looking like its surroundings. Hidden in plain sight. It blended in so well with everything around it. That is the enemy. Hidden in plain sight. Not easily detected, having mastered the way of the chameleon. The closer I looked, the more I could see the subtle movements. The calculated breathing. The slightest slither. He waits. Eyes fixated on his victim, just like the lion. Moving almost undetected until close enough to strike.

YOU SHALL OVERCOME

The lion was different. While the snake barely moved, the lion paced back and forth, never taking his eyes off us. Back and forth. Watching our every move. Waiting for one of us to make the wrong move or fall over into his territory. He stood up tall and proud. His coat was golden and shiny. He was focused yet unintimidated by our presence. He walked as if he knew he was more powerful than us. He walked as if he knew he could defeat us. He walked without fear. It was as if he knew that he was superior to us. Then, he stopped dead in his tracks and let out the most amazing ROAR! We all cheered! "That's it!" I exclaimed. "That's what's in me! That's what Pastor Shavon was talking about!" Boldness is in me! Power is in me! Strength is in me! Superiority is in me! Fearlessness is in me! The level of intense focus is in me! Not only me but you too! But I didn't know that in that bedroom. In that bedroom, the boy was the lion. The boy was superior.

The enemy had a plan for me, for you, for us from the beginning. BUT! My God had a greater plan! You see, in the remainder of John 10:10, the B portion continues with the following encouragement by Jesus Christ Himself: "My purpose is to give them [me, you, us] a rich and satisfying life." Rich and satisfying. I like that!

It was NEVER God's plan for my life for this to happen. But it was His will to protect me in it. It could have been worse. Thank You, Father, for protecting me in it. My Honey always says, "Life is choice-driven." We choose which behaviors we engage in. Although the enemy makes suggestions, the decision is ultimately ours. That boy decided to do what he did to me that day in my brother's bedroom. They decided to do what they did to you. It must be our decision to glorify God despite our experiences. Why? Because it could have been worse.

Be Vigilant

Mothers, fathers, parents, grandparents, PLEASE don't let your guard down. Be present. Be nosy. Be sober. Be vigilant. Be annoying! Although we would like to believe that we can trust the people we allow into our homes, the truth is we just don't know that for sure. All too often, young girls and boys are violated and taken advantage of primarily by those who were family or friends of the family. Take a look at the following statistics regarding child sexual abuse (CSA) provided by the National Center for Victims of Crime:

> **PLEASE DON'T LET YOUR GUARD DOWN. BE PRESENT.**

- 1 in 5 girls and 1 in 20 boys is a victim of child sexual abuse

- Self-report studies show that 20% of adult females and 5-10% of adult males recall a childhood sexual assault or sexual abuse incident
- During one year in the U.S., 16% of youth ages 14 to 17 had been sexually victimized
- Throughout their lifetime, 28% of U.S. youth ages 14 to 17 have been sexually victimized
- Children are most vulnerable to CSA between the ages of 7 and 13.[6]

According to a 2003 National Institute of Justice report, 3 out of 4 adolescents who have been sexually assaulted were victimized by someone they knew well (page 5).[7]

In the vast majority of cases where there is credible evidence that a child has been penetrated, only between 5 and 15% of those children will have genital injuries consistent with sexual abuse.

Child sexual abuse is not solely restricted to physical contact; such abuse could include noncontact abuse, such as exposure, voyeurism, and child pornography.[8]

These statistics are alarming! For so long, I felt as though I was the only one. It was just me. I didn't tell. Reading this chapter will be the first time many in my family have heard about this incident. We must begin to speak up against this wrong being done. We must encourage our children to tell if someone is mistreating, mishandling,

---

6 https://victimsofcrime.org/child-sexual-abuse-statistics
7 https://www.ojp.gov/pdffiles1/nij/194972.pdf
8 https://www.apa.org/pi/families/resources/understanding-child-abuse

touching, or talking to them inappropriately. We must create a safe space for the kids to share their experiences.

> **WE MUST CREATE A SAFE SPACE FOR THE KIDS TO SHARE THEIR EXPERIENCES.**

And TAKE THEM SERIOUSLY! Then, believe them. I read an article written in *Psychology Today* entitled "Why Children Don't Tell Anyone About Sexual Abuse." The article shared five reasons why children don't tell:

- Feelings of guilt, shame, or self-blame
- Fear
- Lack of understanding
- Relationship with the perpetrator
- Gender

I can attest to each of these. This tells me that some conversations need to be had. I never told my parents about this. I never told my brother and sister about this. I didn't know how to start the conversation. I didn't want to get anyone in trouble. Sometimes, telling gets more people in trouble than the one who committed the offense; we have to be okay with that. We have to open up our mouths and not be afraid to speak up and out. Although the conversation will be uncomfortable, empowering them through love will take away the shame of what happened. So many children just bear the burden of what happened and keep silent. They protect, even though they require protection.

I pray that after reading this chapter, you will have a conversation with your child or grandchild, your niece or nephew, brother or sister, or even the neighboring children, if feasible. I pray that you will create that safe space for them to open up about their experiences. It is my prayer that if you have been the victim or even the victimizer, you will also have a conversation about your experiences. Silence kills. The way to overcome this is to speak up and out. Scripture tells us:

> And they overcame and conquered him [the enemy] because of the blood of the Lamb and because of the word of their testimony, for they did not love their life and renounce their faith even when faced with death. (Revelation 12:11 AMP)

Speaking up and out may initially feel like you're dying, but to live, that fear of telling what happened to you must die.

> **A Little Girl's Recommendation:** Teach me the importance and power of my NO. Teach me and demonstrate humility to me. Remind me how valuable I am. Teach me the power and importance of my voice.

My Prayer for Little Girls

Father, I pray for boldness and courage for our little girls. I pray they understand the importance and power of their NO. I pray they are empowered to speak out if someone tries to take advantage of them. I pray they use their voices to speak out against the mistreatment of others. I pray against feelings of guilt, shame, and condemnation. I bind the spirit of fear working against them and loose Your confidence in their lives. I pray against the lack of understanding in our little girls. I pray against the spirit of intimidation that would try to intimidate little girls from speaking out. I pray they don't become part of the statistics of those abused instead of part of those who never experienced maltreatment. In the strong name of Jesus. Amen.

Chapter 4
VIOLATED

Violate–to break, disregard, harm, disrespect, profane, interrupt, disturb.[9]

When someone is violated, they are not just broken; they are shattered. Harm has been done to their person or chastity. They have been disrespected. They have been disregarded. Their peace and well-being have been interrupted and disturbed. They have been damaged. They have been crushed. After being violated, they are discarded. Tossed to the side. Treated as useless and unwanted, leaving them mentally depleted of initiative, vigor, ambition, drive, determination, and will. Violated.

I'm reminded of Tamar, David's daughter, in the Bible. Tamar was a beautiful young woman. The daughter of the king. Protected. Cared for. Provided for. Loved. She was green, chaste, naive. She was oblivious to the danger lurking in the shadows. Youth and unfamiliarity with darkness blinded her from discerning the plot of the enemy against her. In her innocence, she fully trusted her older brother, who was to be a protector. Instead, in her inexperience with the cruelties and depravity in man's heart, she found herself violated. Let's look at what the Bible says about Tamar's experience:

---

9   https://www.merriam-webster.com/dictionary/lust

Now David's son Absalom had a beautiful sister named Tamar. And Amnon, her half-brother, fell desperately in love with her. Amnon became so obsessed with Tamar that he became ill. She was a virgin, and Amnon thought he could never have her. But Amnon had a very crafty friend—his cousin Jonadab. He was the son of David's brother Shimea. One day Jonadab said to Amnon, "What's the trouble? Why should the son of a king look so dejected morning after morning?" So Amnon told him, "I am in love with Tamar, my brother Absalom's sister." "Well," Jonadab said, "I'll tell you what to do. Go back to bed and pretend you are ill. When your father comes to see you, ask him to let Tamar come and prepare some food for you. Tell him you'll feel better if she prepares it as you watch and feeds you with her own hands." So Amnon lay down and pretended to be sick. And when the king came to see him, Amnon asked him, "Please let my sister Tamar come and cook my favorite dish as I watch. Then I can eat it from her own hands." So David agreed and sent Tamar to Amnon's house to prepare some food for him. When Tamar arrived at Amnon's house, she went to the place where he was lying down so he could watch her mix some dough. Then she baked his favorite dish for him. But when she set the serving tray before him, he refused to eat. "Everyone get out of here," Amnon told his servants. So, they all left. Then he said to Tamar, "Now bring the food into my bedroom and feed it to me here." So Tamar took his favorite dish to him. But as she was feeding him, he grabbed her and demanded, "Come to bed with me, my darling sister." "No, my brother!" she cried. "Don't be foolish! Don't do this to me! Such wicked things aren't done in Israel. Where could I go in my shame? And you would be called one of the greatest fools in Israel. Please, just speak to the king about it, and he will let you marry me." But Amnon wouldn't listen to her, and since he was stronger than she was, he raped her. Then suddenly Amnon's love turned to hate, and he hated her even more than he had loved her. "Get out of here!" he snarled at her. "No, no!" Tamar cried. "Sending me away now is worse than what you've already done to me." But Amnon wouldn't listen to her. He shouted for his servant and demanded, "Throw this woman out, and lock the door behind her!" So the servant put her out and locked the door behind her. She was wearing a long, beautiful robe, as was the custom in those days for the king's virgin daughters. But now Tamar tore her robe and put ashes on her head. And then, with her face in her hands, she went away crying. (2 Samuel 13:1-19 NLT)

The unfortunate familiarity of Tamar's story saddens me. Did you see how her brother took counsel from his demented friend and deceived the King all to fulfill a lustful desire? His lust led him to disrespect, disregard, harm, abuse, desecrate, pollute, and defile his sister! Then, after the lustful desire was satisfied, he discarded her as if she were a worthless piece of trash.

When lust is left unchecked, it leads us down a path of destruction. Merriam-Webster defines lust as usually intense or unbridled sexual desire. Amnon had no restraint. He had his heart set on conquering Tamar. He completely disregarded her feelings and failed to adhere to her plea not to go forward with something so heinous. He took advantage of her and baited her into his bedroom. He pretended to be physically sick yet exposed the fact that he was spiritually sick and mentally depraved. Then, he treated her as though she were nothing afterward. Any man or woman who will go to such lengths to overpower and take advantage of someone needs deliverance.

When I first encountered her story in scripture, my mind took me back to the 1980s. We had hurriedly moved from Los Angeles to Bakersfield. Because the apartment was jam-packed with people, we played outside often. Unlike today, we didn't have computers, cell phones, and video games to occupy our minds and time. We made up games to play. We played outside all day!

On Saturday mornings, my Grammie would wake us up early. After washing our faces and brushing our teeth, we would have breakfast. Usually, during the hot months, we ate cold cereal and during the cold months, we would eat hot cereal. Then we did our chores while Grammie made us a bag lunch. She would pack each of us a sandwich, a piece of fruit, and one of those small red boxes of raisins. She didn't need to pack a drink because we would drink from the water fountain.

Once our chores were done, we would go to the park and stay all day long! We didn't dare leave the park. We knew better. Grammie was a strict disciplinarian, and none of us wanted to get a whooping. We played games like Hide-and-Seek, Freeze Tag, and Duck, Duck, Goose. We would make mud pies and homemade slip-and-slides and play in the sprinklers to get wet on hot days.

While at the park one Saturday, he said we were going to the playhouse. He said he would be the daddy, and I would be the mommy. Nothing happened at the park that day, but I now realize it was a prelude to what would happen later that night. He was preparing me mentally for what was to come later, you know, for what grown-ups did when it was dark. I hated being in Bakersfield because I was away from Dad, but I liked it when we all played outside together because I felt safe. Nighttime was different though.

Monster Unmasked

No one knew the boogie man was living with us. No one knew there was a monster living with us. No one knew a predator was living with us. He was hidden in plain sight. He looked just like the other kids. Normal. Unsuspecting. That's how cunning, conniving and subtle the enemy is. The Bible suggests with vivid description:

> **NO ONE KNEW THE BOOGIE MAN WAS LIVING WITH US.**

> Now the serpent was more subtle than any beast of the field which the LORD God had made.
>
> (Genesis 3:1)

He's sneaky.

A master of disguise.

A chameleon.

No one knew the safety the sunrise provided me nor the danger sunset presented me. While it was daytime, I was surrounded by my brother and other cousins, sticking close to them for protection. They had no clue. While I'm sure my presence annoyed them, their presence provided a respite from abuse. So, wherever they were, I was. Whatever they did, I did. They were my safe space during the day and some nights. So, if they stayed out past sunset, I was right there. I felt there was no other choice. I knew that sunset was the curfew. However, to prolong the inevitable, the punishment of violating curfew was worth it. Punishment also provided protection. Some nights, I even stayed up late with the others just so I could escape the clutches of the enemy, hoping he would fall asleep before I did.

For quite some time, sunsets were beautifully scary. I loved to see the beautiful array of colors in the sky at dusk but hated what happened after the sun hid itself. The clouds would turn different shades of orange and pink against the setting sun. I often found myself lost in daydreaming about what life would be like if what I was facing wasn't my reality. I can see myself now dancing and singing on the clouds as if they were my stage. Singing my little heart out as if I could sing… lol. I loved the way the birds looked as they glided across the skies as the sun slowly faded out of sight.

Today, I love to sit on the pier or in the sand at the beach and watch the sunset. It is one of the most beautiful sights! Today, for me, there is no fear associated with the sun setting. It's no longer scary. The Lord did make the earth beautiful. In my adult, mature state, I appreciate the beauty of the sunset. However, in my adolescence, that was not the case. Then, the sun rose and set. It was like safety appearing and disappearing time and again. After dark, something sinister would happen, and it would happen often.

> **I HAD BECOME THE GAME. MY BODY HAD BECOME HIS PLAYGROUND.**

Occasionally, during the day, he would cop a feel here and there. You know, sneak it in, in plain sight, as if challenging his prowess. Looking back, I can see now how he was growing more and more bold, feeling superior to me. His confidence increased with each successful touch, rub, and squeeze. But after dark, there were no holds barred. His hands would be all over the most sacred and private parts of my body without permission as if I were his property.

During the day, when we played outside, I would always be the one he wanted to seek when playing Hide-n-Seek. I would always be the one he wanted to chase and tag when playing Tag or Freeze Tag. I would always end up being the one his hand landed on, especially when playing Duck, Duck Goose. He wanted me to chase him.

I hated chasing him. It made him feel like I wanted him, like I desired him and yearned for what he had grown so comfortable doing to me. In his mind, I was a willing participant in what was repeatedly occurring. It was completely lost upon him that I lacked the mental maturity to consent to such activity. Nonetheless, I was the target. I had become the game. My body had become his playground.

How could he do this to me? Didn't he know he was hurting me? He carried on like he had not a care in the world while I lay terrified, powerless, defeated. I screamed as loud as I could. Why wasn't anyone listening? Why didn't they come to rescue me? Can't they hear me screaming? Although loud in my head and loud in my heart, no sound left my mouth.

Over, over, and over. Time after time after time. I hated what was happening, but I was so helpless. I was so weak. I was so tiny. Time dragged by. It seemed like it went on forever. I never got used to it. I was never prepared for it. I never wanted it. I often hoped someone would come in and catch him. I cried silently and tried my best to stay away from him. I tried to avoid him. I tried to stay out of his reach. However, in a good ole predatory fashion, he hunted me down. He always kept his eyes on me. It seemed as though no matter where I went, he was there. Watching. Waiting.

Somehow, he always found a way to get next to me. Somehow, he always found just room enough to slither his way into my space. I couldn't fight him off. He was too big. He was too strong. He was too powerful. If I tattled, who would believe me? If I spoke up, who would listen? So, I just endured. Night after night, I endured. Molestation after molestation, I endured. Violation after violation. I endured.

The Pattern Changed

I remember the last time like it was yesterday. He must have gotten bold because, this time, the sun was up. It was early on a Saturday morning. Grammie had awakened us early as usual. We had a weekend routine. However, this time was different. Instead of following the routine we always followed on Saturday mornings, he was lying on his side, and he made me sit in front of him on the edge of the bed, with my feet dangling from the side. He had the cover over his body and partially over mine. His nasty hands were moving methodically over my body as they had done so many times before. My eyes were tightly closed. My mind was racing. My heart was pounding inside my chest.

I resisted mentally.

Emotionally, I was confused.

I screamed inwardly.

It was Saturday morning. He never hurt me on Saturday morning, or any other morning for that matter. He was a night terror; The darkness was his hiding place. He had mastered midnight. But he was an opportunist. That has Satan written all over it!

> **HE WAS A NIGHT TERROR; THE DARKNESS WAS HIS HIDING PLACE.**

Satan lurks in the shadows, studying his prey and the environment intently. He patiently awaits the prime opportunity to strike. He observes patterns and proclivities. He studies weaknesses and shortcomings. He is an expert strategist! I say this not to credit the enemy in any fashion but rather to open our eyes to just how calculated he is.

He Needs to Be Exposed!

He is so crafty and sick that he uses young boys to violate young girls. He uses our vulnerabilities against us. He weaponizes our weaknesses. With each passing opportunity, he slithers slightly closer, and once he is within the strike zone, he launches forward and latches on, injecting us with his venom, unsuspectingly and momentarily paralyzing us, leaving our heads spinning and wondering, "What in the World Just Happened?"

Naturally speaking, severe pain, redness, and swelling surround the place of impact. One may also notice blistering and tenderness. As the poison travels through the body of the victim, their breathing becomes labored and difficult. This is how I felt. Like I was suffocating. Like I was slowly dying. I didn't know how much more of this abuse I could take. I wanted it to stop so badly.

Grammie! Please help me!

A once outgoing, playful, innocent little girl, I was now withdrawn, timid, and even sheepish. I had become afraid of the nighttime, horrified of what happens when the sun sets and the lights go out. I had been violated.

Often, I would think, "Am I the only one? Are there others out there who are experiencing this?" All grown up, I know that I wasn't the only one. There are many of me out there. I have had many conversations with men, women, and children who have shared their encounters with me. I cry inside. They cry outside. Sometimes, we just hug and cry together. We must bring awareness to this dark evil plaguing our children. We must open our mouths and speak up! I pray this book empowers you to speak out. We have been in these secrets long enough.

Last Dance with Darkness

The door swung open! Grammie busted him right in the act! FINALLY! I was excited and scared at the same time. The enemy tried to convince me that I welcomed and wanted what was happening to me. So, when Grammie busted in, I was scared that I was going to get in trouble. I was afraid I was doing something wrong. This is how the enemy does us. He violates us and then makes us feel like what we experienced was our fault. He blames the victim. He makes us feel like *we* were wrong and the one who violated us was right. For this cause, many remain silent. Slowly deteriorating inside from the poison of defilement and violation. Not today. Not anymore. Today, we break free. Today, we OVERCOME.

> I WAS AFRAID I WAS DOING SOMETHING WRONG.

A myriad of emotions flooded Grammie's face. She looked mortified at what she was seeing. He and I were startled. I jumped up quickly, crying. Grammie angrily shouted, "What the **** is going on in here?" Grammie was heated! It's almost as if all the color drained from her face. She continued, "Boy, get your..." "Maxine, get me that **** broom!" I had never been so excited to get a broom in all my life! I had a child-sized straw broom set that I played with as a little girl. The broom handle was a pretty green color. It was about 36" long and maybe an inch in diameter. When Grammie swept the floor with her big broom, I would mimic her with my little broom. This time, Grammie wouldn't be sweeping the floor. My little broom was the closest, so I handed her that one. In her disgust and anger, she snatched the broom from me and began to exact punishment on him.

Finally, retribution had come. I cheered her on silently. Blow after blow. Scream after scream! Go, Grammie go! Get him! She punished him so hard and so long that my little broom snapped in half! That's when she stopped. I wished she would have kept going. He cried frantically. Grammie sweated profusely and breathed heavily. I looked on in horror and honor, feeling vindicated. "Don't you bring yo' ****** out this room! Maxine, come with me." We left the room together, leaving him to himself.

"Maxine, come with me" was the extent of the conversation about what Grammie had witnessed and what I had endured for so long. It was never mentioned verbally again. Grammie spoke to me with action. From that time forward, I slept in bed with her. She kept me closer to her than before. Now, where she went, I went. What she did, I did. She didn't say any words about it, but her actions were VERY LOUD.

A Little Girl's Recommendation: When I come to you, please listen to me. Please don't disregard my feelings. Please remind me of my worth. I would love for us to spend quality time together.

My Prayer for Little Girls

Father, I pray for little girls to have a safe space to share their experiences. I pray that when they have the courage to speak out, the one they speak to has the wisdom to listen. I pray for the sensitivity of parents to hear little girls when they speak about what's bothering them. I pray for the courage of parents to remove little girls from hurtful situations. I pray they are kept from harmful situations. I pray they are kept from dangerous situations. I pray, Father, that You guard them from manipulative people, places, and situations. I pray little girls aren't blinded to those who pose a threat to them. In Jesus' name. Amen.

Chapter 5
IT WAS BIGGER THAN THAT

In the days following the incident, things seemed to be getting back to normal. Though I was finally free from the monster that lurked in the shadows of the nighttime, I wished Grammie and I would have had that conversation. I had so many questions. I wanted to know why he did what he did. I wanted to know why he chose me. I wanted to know if I was the only one. I wanted to know so much. But we never had a conversation. I was just glad that it was over. I didn't suffer any more physical abuse at the hands of my cousin since Grammie caught him and beat him.

Over time, I was able to go play with the other kids. It was as if we had forgotten all about what had taken place. My battle, however, would be far from over, although the physical abuse ceased. The mental torment and anguish were amplified.

I wanted to talk about what happened. I needed to talk about what happened. On the other hand, I was too frightened to bring it up. I wasn't taught how to initiate conversations and communicate with adults. We were taught to "stay in a child's place" and to "speak when spoken to." We were taught to "stay out of grown folks' business" and that "what happens in this house stays in this house."

Drowning in Silence

I didn't have a voice. My voice was taken from me before I was even old enough to understand the art of communication. I wasn't given a safe space to share my feelings and experiences. The safest space for what happened to me was inside me, and I suffocated and suffered as a result.

Grammie dealt with the situation the best way she could. Even though she rescued me from the physical clutches of the enemy, more was necessary. I felt like the victim of a drowning. It was as if I was submerged underwater for longer than my air supply would allow, struggling to keep my airway clear of water. I felt like I held my breath as long as I could. I felt like I had begun aspirating, and my lungs had started to fill up with water.

Eventually, I went unconscious. The moment when I lost consciousness was the moment Grammie beat down the door and barged in. She pulled me out of deep waters and lay me in a safe place. However, not having the conversation I desperately needed to have was like that drowning victim being pulled out of the water and not administered CPR. The purpose of CPR is to get and keep oxygenated blood flowing through the body and to the brain. Without this flow of blood and oxygen, the person could end up in cardiac arrest and eventually die. I was only partially rescued.

Looking back, I realize this wasn't just a physical experience. It was a whole being experience. My mind was violated. My emotions were violated. My thought patterns were violated. My perception of protection, love, and trust was altered, and it showed up in the days, weeks, months, and years to come.

Just One of the Boys

I no longer trusted boys. I no longer saw them as protection. I saw them as the enemy. Because the enemy used a young boy, now, in my mind, all the other boys were like my cousin. They all preyed on young girls. To protect myself from the boys, I began to act like them. I carried myself like them. I talked like them. As time went on, my mannerisms were like the boys.

I preferred to hang out with boys because my idea about girls had also been shaped. Because I was too afraid, weak, and powerless to do anything about what my cousin was doing to me, I saw other girls as afraid, weak, and powerless too. I didn't want to associate myself with weakness, so I didn't hang out with little girls.

I associated the boys with power. I hung out with and associated with what I perceived to be powerful. This is how I empowered myself. This was my defense mechanism. I knew the boys I hung out with weren't into boys. My logic was that if I became one of the guys, I would be safe. I reasoned that if I acted like them, talked like them, walked like them, dressed like them, and carried myself like them, they would see me as one of them and not as a young girl. They would no longer desire me. Consequently, I became one of them. I became a tomboy.

I was in an identity crisis. In my mind, it was impossible to be who God created me to be. That person was fragile, powerless, and incapable of protecting herself. That person was easily overpowered, lacking the ability to fight back. As a tomboy, that was not the case. I saw myself differently. I saw myself as strong and capable. When I learned how to fight and fight good, that became my resolution to all the problems that came later. I knew I was good at it, so it became my "go-to." Fighting became my norm. Not talking. Not reasoning. Fighting.

Seeds of Suspicion

This issue with how I now see males would prove to be one of the biggest barriers in my relationship with God. Today, I realized this was the plan of the enemy all along. It was never about my dad not being there. It was never about him abandoning me. It was never about him not fighting for me. It was never about being violated. It was never about being taken advantage of. It was never about an identity crisis. It was never about fighting. Those were all part of the greater scheme of me not trusting God as Father.

Father. A male. A man. Masculine. Here's the connection. If I didn't trust males, I wouldn't be able to trust God as a Father. The enemy went to great lengths to alter my perception of male figures just so I wouldn't receive God as The Father and male figure He is. The plan was that my trust issues would be so deep-rooted that when it came for God to reveal Himself to me through His Son Jesus, I would reject Him because He was male.

> **IF I DIDN'T TRUST MALES, I WOULDN'T BE ABLE TO TRUST GOD AS A FATHER.**

On my journey, I discovered that the trust issues I had with men carried over to my relationship with God. I found it hard to trust Him because of them. By the enemy's design, I had attributed experiences with men to God. I had put God on the same plane as man, thus making it almost impossible to fully trust Him.

When The Father revealed this to me, I was taken aback. At first, I could not make the connection between the two, but then I began to examine how I interacted with God, His Son, and His Word. I found some things in the Word easier to trust than others. The blessings and provisions were easy to trust. Even the consequences of unbelief were easy to trust. However, it was difficult for me to see God as my Father because my father left me. My father abandoned me. My father fell short of protecting me and fighting for me. My father failed me. I could not see God as a father because I already had one of them who, in my mind, didn't want to be that. Allowing God to be The Father to me that He desired to be would require me to trust Him, and I just couldn't do that and risk being abandoned again. I couldn't risk being left again. I couldn't risk not being protected again. So, I only allowed God in partially, just short of the "Father" part.

Challenge Accepted

I remembered the day God freed me. My mentor and I had embarked on a 30-day, 5:00 a.m., 1-hour-long prayer challenge. The challenge was to pray daily for at least one hour for thirty consecutive days. One morning, God freed me from the trust issue I was having with Him being Father to me.

I had gone into my office and lay face down on the floor as I had done many mornings before. I can still smell the carpet. A blanket was spread beneath me, and another throw was spread on top of me. It was a cold morning. My arms were folded and crossed. My forehead rested on my arms. It wasn't daylight savings yet, so the room was pitch black. No one was home but me. Everything was quiet. Not even the sound of cars whizzing by on the streets could be heard.

I began thanking God for life, health, and strength. I began thanking Him for all He has provided. I offered up adoration to Him, telling Him how wonderful He is and how I appreciated Him for who He is in my life. I began to thank Him for my husband, children, and leaders. I asked Him to forgive me for any sins, iniquities, and transgressions. I asked Him to create in me a clean heart and to renew the right spirit in me. I asked Him to search my heart and to uproot anything in me that was not like Him. I asked Him to reveal anything I was harboring in my heart. This is when the issue of my father came up.

The Search Was Over

I remember times when I would pray to find my father. I can remember sitting and daydreaming about whether he was still alive. I often found myself wondering if he had other children. Do I have other brothers and sisters? Where do they live? What do they look like? Do they know about me? Are they wondering the same thing about me? I searched on social media. I searched online. Nothing. Outwardly, I wasn't concerned and didn't care. Inwardly, there was a hole.

But *that* morning, face down on the floor, I asked God if I should continue to search for my father. Should I pursue it or let it go? The Lord began to minister to me. He told me to let it go.

"I am your Father. He was just the vessel I used to get you here. I've been your father all along. I've been there all along. He played the role I needed him to play, and when that role was done, I allowed the separation. Now I need you to trust Me as your Father."

> **FATHER, I DON'T KNOW HOW TO TRUST YOU.**

I was crying so much as I listened attentively with my spirit.

Father, I don't know how to trust You. The last father I trusted abandoned me. The last father I trusted didn't protect me." I was crying so hard at the reality of what was in my heart. Hearing myself tell God that I didn't trust Him hurt me. I mean, how could I not trust Him? He had been so good to me! Yet, in my heart, I was withholding my trust. "I want to trust You, but I'm scared. I'm scared to trust You."

Imagine pouring your heart out to The Father, who has always been there. I was honest enough to tell Him that I wanted to trust Him but was afraid to. I had trusted a father before, but that trust was betrayed.

"I'm not like man," He said.

"I'm scared."

"You can trust Me." I cried harder.

"I'll trust You, but please don't leave me. Please don't abandon me. Please don't walk away from me."

I found myself begging and pleading with God not to do the thing He said He wouldn't do. I had placed God in the same category as man. I had treated God as if He were the one who abandoned me. I had withheld my trust from Him as if He were the one who betrayed me. My lips declared my trust, but my heart said something different.

This was the enemy's plan, which he put in motion years ago. He strategically uses people, situations, and circumstances to plant seeds of mistrust in our hearts. The enemy knows that if we ever get to the place of truly trusting God, he will no longer be able to control us.

God Is Not a Man

I lay on the floor that morning and wept and wept. I cried so much that my eyes hurt. The memory of that morning still brings tears to my eyes. I now cry tears of joy and gratitude because My Father loves me so much that even when I didn't want to trust Him, He didn't give up on me. He allowed me to see how it was the enemy who was at work. Even in doubt, He reassured me. I love Him even more for that. Family, I encourage you to allow God into those spaces you have kept guarded for so long. I encourage you to open up and trust Him fully. He truly is trustworthy. Look at what the Bible says about who God is.

> God is not a man, so he does not lie. He is not human, so he does not change his mind. Has he ever spoken and failed to act? Has he ever promised and not carried it through? (Numbers 23:19 NLT)

Now, "GOD IS NOT A MAN" is a constant reminder that no matter when or where man fails, GOD IS NOT A MAN. He will NEVER fail. He is incapable of failing. Man is flawed and prone to falling short and failing, but GOD IS NOT A MAN. This fact alone is why the Word of God admonishes us not to trust in man.

> It is better to trust in the LORD Than to put confidence in man. (Psalm 118:8)

> Blessed is the man that trusteth in the LORD, and whose hope the LORD is. For he shall be as a tree planted by the waters, and that spreadeth out her roots by the river, and shall not see when heat cometh, but her leaf shall be green; and shall not be careful in the year of drought, neither shall cease from yielding fruit.
> (Jeremiah 17:7-8)

The enemy wants to rob us of our confidence in God. He wants to muddy the waters, rendering us incapable of clearly seeing God for the loving Father He truly is. He wants to keep us in a cycle of distrust. This morning, I realized I was missing out. I was missing out on the experience and encounter He desired me to have with Him.

> **THE ENEMY WANTS TO ROB US OF OUR CONFIDENCE IN GOD.**

So, I have a few questions for you:

- What experiences and encounters with God are you missing out on?

- Are you truly trusting God, or have you allowed situations, circumstances, and experiences with man to stop you from trusting Him?
- Where is that line of demarcation?
- Where have you stopped trusting Him?

As you take time to think about the answers, I encourage you to be open and honest about what's been the barrier to you fully trusting God. Let's take it a step further. I challenge you to surrender that barrier to God and allow Him in further than you have before today.

> **A Little Girl's Recommendation:** Raise me to know and trust God. Teach me who I am as a little girl, becoming a young woman. Help me understand what it means to be in an identity crisis.

My Prayer for Little Girls

Father, I pray You reveal Yourself to little girls and that they come to know You and trust You at a young age. I pray they find their identity in You. I pray against every strategy of the enemy against little girls that would cause them to question their identity. I pray for little girls to be confident in who You made them. I pray they know early on that they don't have to compete with who the world says they should be. I pray they find peace in who You made them and how you made them. I pray the lines for them never be blurred. I pray You are the only one they seek to impress. I pray Your attention is the only attention they crave. I pray Your affirmation of them is the only affirmation they long for. I pray Your endless love for them is the only love they seek to know. In Jesus' name. Amen.

Chapter 6
I AM NOT WHAT HAPPENED TO ME

Mature–having attained a final desired state fully developed, well-balanced, level-headed in identity, temperament, and demonstrative conduct; complete. Perfect.[10]

"This is just who I am." Have you ever said that when your behavior, character, or personality was challenged? I have, several times, when I wasn't willing and ready to accept the provocation to change. The truth is the mannerisms I displayed were manifestations of who I had become, who I had taught myself to be. Deeper, my behavior was a mirror reflecting the condition of my heart. I had not grown to a place where I could be honest with myself and declare, "Regardless of what happened, you have a say in how you conduct yourself." I had not arrived at the destination of maturation.

Maturity is God's designated and desired destination for His creation. Maturation in the spirit. Maturation in the Word of God. Maturity in the Kingdom of God. Observe what the Bible says about spiritual maturation:

---

10   https://www.merriam-webster.com/dictionary/mature

> Consider it a sheer gift, friends, when tests and challenges come at you from all sides. You know that under pressure, your faith life is forced into the open and shows its true colors. So don't try to get out of anything prematurely. Let it do its work so you become mature and well-developed, not deficient in any way.
>
> (James 1:2-4 MSG)

Maturity highlights the attributes and characteristics of a mature person. "I am not what happened to me" is a declaration of maturity. This proclamation not only acknowledges what happened but realizes that it was an isolated incident at a moment in time that cannot be altered. I professed, "I do not identify as what happened. I am not defined by what happened. I am in no way hindered by what happened." This affirmation highlights the work in my heart performed by the Master Craftsman.

For some, "I am not what happened to me" will be the opening announcement in your journey of overcoming. For others, "I am not what people happened to me" will be the encouragement necessary to get through some of the toughest and darkest moments. Yet, for others, "I am not what happened to me" will be the bell ringing after crossing the finish line of the most challenging lap in this race to overcome! At this juncture in my journey, "I am not what happened to me" is the victory dance marking the end of years-long mental affliction, agony, anguish, persecution, misery, and suffering. However, this avouchment has appeared at pivotal points in my journey.

But Ready

As I reminisce about some of the most trying times in my journey of overcoming, I'm reminded of a moment when I stood looking at myself in the mirror. Eyes bloodshot red, puffy, and sore. Face drenched with tears. Head pounding uncontrollably from the pressure. Trying to muster up the courage and strength to tell myself, "I am not what happened to me." Trying to convince myself. Another futile attempt to persuade myself. Thinking, "You got this Max. You're bigger than what happened. You're stronger than what happened. Now is the time to take back the power that what happened has over you!" I was ready. Crying and ready. Eyes swollen and red, but ready. Feeling as though my head had been run over by a semi, but ready.

I opened my mouth to speak, but nothing came out. Have you ever been there? Have you ever been in a place where, in your mind, you know all the right things to say? Just the way to say it? And when the time comes to say what you have rehearsed in your mind, nothing comes out? How frustrating!

> **I OPENED MY MOUTH TO SPEAK, BUT NOTHING CAME OUT.**

"Breathe Max." I breathed in long and deep, then exhaled slowly, expelling all the oxygen out of my lungs. Again. Inhale deeply. Exhale slowly. "Stay calm. You can do this." Sometimes, you must talk yourself through some things. There will be times when we are our biggest cheerleader, our greatest hype-man. The breathing exercises did not help. They were supposed to calm me, but I found myself increasing in anger. I aggressively wiped my face in disgust. "YOU GOT THIS!" I reprimanded myself. "GET IT TOGETHER!" I stood up straight. Squared my shoulders. Tilted my chin up slightly. Looked at myself eye to eye. Braced myself on the counter and leaned in a bit. I opened my mouth, but nothing came out. "UGH! WHAT IS WRONG WITH YOU?"

Am I the only one who is unnaturally hard on myself? Why are we like that? Why do we give others more grace than we are willing to give ourselves? In my mind, there was no excuse for this inability to articulate something so simple. I mean, when did I begin having issues saying what was on my mind? Being outspoken has NEVER been a problem. Now, suddenly, nothing will come out. I reprimanded myself yet again. Growling in anger, "WHAT IS WRONG WITH YOU? STOP BEING SOFT! GET! IT! TOGETHER!" What was happening to me? Why won't anything come out? UGH!

I stood there. Barely able to make out the silhouette of the person before me due to the tears. I was fuming! My palms were sweaty. My heart was racing. With tightly clenched fists, through gritted teeth, and with much strain, I stared myself down in that mirror and growled, "I - am - not - what - happened - to - me." I had to FIGHT to get those words out!

I paused after each word, pressing to complete the statement. They were buried deep down inside me, just waiting for an opening to escape. Looking for the opportunity to break free. Those words were trapped deep down and held hostage for years! Pain refusing to let them go. Hurt refusing to let them go. Anger refusing to let them go. Confusion refusing to let them go. Betrayal refusing to let them go.

When we, despite what happened, declare something as powerful as "I am not what happened to me," we obliterate the obstructions, demolish the deterrents, and break the barriers holding our deliverance captive! But! They had to let me go! I let out several blood-curdling screams and fell to the floor, curled up into a fetal position, and rocked back and forth, sobbing uncontrollably. Through sniffs repeating "I am not what happened to me. I am not what happened to me. I am not what happened to me." No one was there. No one to comfort me. No one to console me. No one to hug me. No one to tell me it's going to be alright. No one.

Process and Protection

Now I realize that in this life there will be some situations we have to walk through alone. The noise and chatter of others can sometimes hinder the work God desires to do in us. So, He has to get us in a place where we can be still and hear His voice clearly without outside interference. This is part of the maturation process.

At some point, we must let go of the hand we are so used to holding and begin to walk on our own. This was one of those times for me. On the surface, it appeared as though it should not have been that difficult nor taken that long to make that confession. However, that confession had to come from below the surface. It had to come from the heart.

When we have been violated, fractured, neglected, broken, or betrayed, our hearts do not recover from the trauma without actively and persistently pursuing restoration. The heart records the trauma and immediately begins to devise a plan of protection. This protection may show up in the form of rudeness, disregard for others, being standoffish, anger, lashing out, building walls, introversion, etc. All of these are defense mechanisms to protect the heart from further traumatic experiences.

> **ALL OF THESE ARE DEFENSE MECHANISMS TO PROTECT THE HEART.**

Because the heart does not know how to function when faced with such strain, it shuts down, it shuts out, and it shuts off.

My heart, to protect itself from further trauma, shut people down, shut people out, and shut itself off from caring and feeling as it was originally designed.

My heart had been blackened by the poison of what happened. This poison spread throughout my heart and choked the life out of it. My heart died. It was no longer alive to the original design of God.

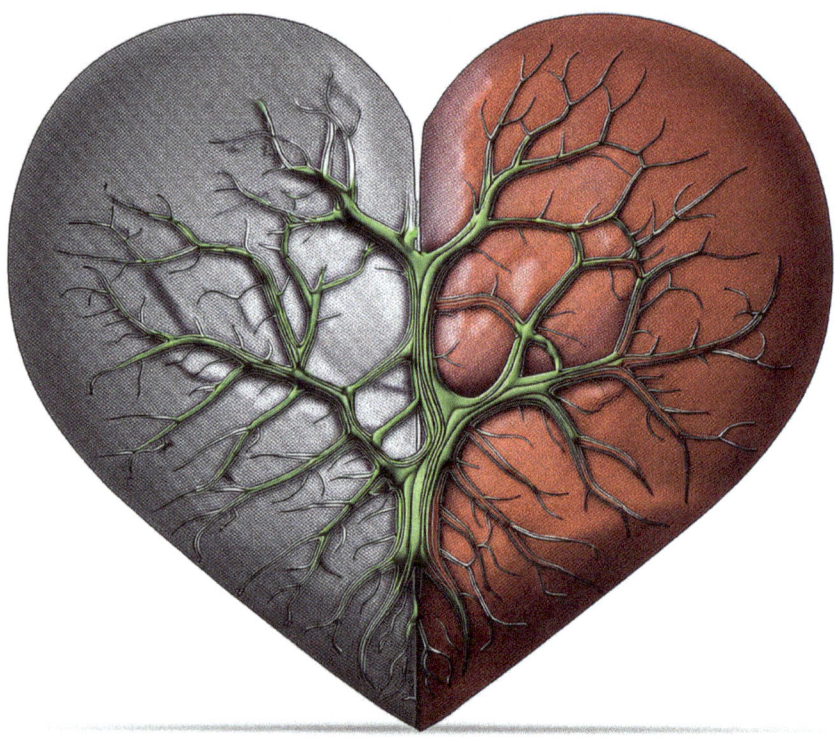

I hated people. I hated people because of what one person did to me. I hated myself because of what happened to me. I hated life, so I lived extremely recklessly. Any confessions of light and life were buried so deep in my heart that when freedom called out to me, I had to fight hard to get it. That day in that mirror was Round 1.

I desired freedom.

I had grown weary of carrying around all the anger, hatred, and bitterness. I wanted and needed to experience the love I was supposed to feel. Love was ripped out of me when I was a young girl. The violation I suffered at the hands of my cousin extracted any residue of love left in me. I wanted what was mine.

My Encounter

Paul, in his first letter to the church at Corinth, shared this powerful truth:

> Love endures with patience and serenity, love is kind and thoughtful, and is not jealous or envious; love does not brag and is not proud or arrogant. It is not rude; it is not self-seeking, it is not provoked [nor overly sensitive and easily angered]; it does not take into account a wrong endured. It does not rejoice at injustice, but rejoices with the truth [when right and truth prevail]. Love bears all things [regardless of what comes], believes all things [looking for the best in each one], hopes all things [remaining steadfast during difficult times], endures all things [without weakening]. Love never fails [it never fades nor ends].
> (1 Corinthians 13:4-8 AMP)

Love is what was missing. Love for God. Love for His Son. Love For His presence. Love for myself. I had to love myself enough to want to be free. When freedom showed up, love showed up. The enemy does not want us to love The Father nor receive His love.

> **WHEN FREEDOM SHOWED UP, LOVE SHOWED UP.**

He knows the love of God supersedes situations and circumstances. I didn't have love because I didn't know love. Can you identify with this? Can you say for certain that you have love and have met love? John received a powerful revelation from God about love:

> Dear friends, let us continue to love one another, for love comes from God. Anyone who loves is a child of God and knows God. God showed how much he loved us by sending his one and only Son into the world so that we might have eternal life through him. This is real love—not that we loved God, but that he loved us and sent his Son as a sacrifice to take away our sins. (1 John 4:7, 9-10 NLT)

It was my encounter with love that enabled me to declare, "I am not what happened to me."

A Little Girl's Recommendation: Talk to me about the significance of not allowing things I experience to become my identity. Teach me how to articulate my emotions. Can we play board games and plant flowers together?

My Prayer for Little Girls

Father, I thank You for loving little girls. I thank You that they are precious in Your eyes. I thank You for Your unfailing love towards them. I thank You for Your sustaining love towards them. I thank You that though they may be too young to comprehend the depth of Your love for them, Your love never falters. I thank You Father that Your love for little girls is sure, constant, certain. And I thank You Father for the pure love You have placed in their hearts. I thank You Father for expressing Your love for them to them in a way they can understand. I thank You for the power to overcome You have placed on the inside of them. I thank You for their innate knowledge of right and wrong. I thank You Father for the introduction of Your Son, which is the most powerful expression of Your love for not just little girls, but for all of us. In Jesus' Name, I pray. Amen.

Chapter 7
CONTINUE TO FIGHT

Fight–To strive or contend for victory, in battle or single combat; to attempt to defeat, subdue, or destroy an enemy, either by blows or weapons; to contend in arms.[11]

Before surrendering my life to Christ, fighting was the only way I knew how to express myself. Sometimes I fought using words and at other times, I fought with silence. However, the majority of the fights were with my hands, feet, or whatever I could pick up. Fighting was how I was taught to resolve issues. I was shaped into fighting.

I remember the first fight I ever had. I was around four years old. There was this little girl who lived in the apartment complex. We were friends. We played together all the time. She was so pretty and light-skinned. She was nice to me. She never tried to boss me around or bully me. We played together almost every day when we were allowed to play outside. She brought her baby dolls, and I brought mine. We shared our toys with one another like little girls do.

We would play on the stairs or underneath the stairs. Sometimes we would make mud pies or mud burgers out of the dirt, or tacos

---

[11] https://av1611.com/kjbp/kjv-dictionary/fight.html

and burritos using the leaves from the plants as the shells, while other times we would push our toy grocery baskets around and pretend as though we were grocery shopping.

The courtyard in the apartment complex seemed massive! Grocery shopping would take forever, lol. The walkways doubled as the aisles in our makeshift grocery store. To our tiny bodies and short legs, the walk around the grocery store seemed endless. The scenery was beautiful, though. The plants were a dark, beautiful green hue. The flowers were always in bloom. Large stones were strategically placed to create an amazing landscape.

I can still smell the smell of chlorine in the swimming pool. The pool was situated amid foliage and masonry. We didn't know how to swim yet, and the pool had a gate around it, so the pool was off-limits. The courtyard, however, was ours though. We utilized every accessible square inch during our play times. The giggles, laughter, and singing of little girls filled the atmosphere.

The First Fight

One day, that all changed. I don't recall the details surrounding the fight, but I vividly remember the altercation. Before this day, I had no formal combat training, nor did I need it. I was just a baby in the eyes of the adults. To my brother and sister, I was more of a brat and nuisance. I was inexperienced in fighting, unlearned, and very much a novice.

My heart was racing at what seemed like a hundred miles per hour! One thing led to another and before I knew it, we were in an all-out brawl. I grabbed her with both hands by the shirt on her chest and began to rub my hands together as if I were scrubbing a piece of laundry between them. To me, I was giving it all I had while she simultaneously hit me with all the strength she could muster up.

Thinking back on that day, I laugh out loud. But at that moment, I was afraid. I was afraid to fight. I was afraid of losing my friend. I was afraid of losing. I was afraid of getting beaten up. I was afraid of being laughed at. I was afraid of disappointing my brother. I looked up to him. I wanted to do everything he did. I wanted to be everywhere he was. I wanted to know how to fight like he knew how to fight.

To my ridicule, shame, and disappointment, my brother laughed at me. He laughed hysterically at my defensive prowess, or lack thereof, and mocked me repeatedly. I never told him how much his mockery bothered me. He never knew how small, insignificant, and inadequate his reaction made me feel.

I decided at that moment that I would never be scorned again for not knowing how to fight. I don't know that I lost that fight. But if I did, I do know that it was the first and last time I felt inferior in fighting, though it would be a while before I would be faced with an opportunity to highlight my talent in another bout.

> **I WOULD NEVER BE SCORNED AGAIN FOR NOT KNOWING HOW TO FIGHT.**

Combat Academy

As time went on, I would play fights with my brother, boy cousins, and their friends. I wasn't very tall, so they would get on their knees, coming down to my level to fight with me and teach me how to maneuver. I really enjoyed this! I especially liked it when we slap-boxed. They were always quicker, bigger, stronger, and slapped way harder than me. This motivated me to try harder to win.

Occasionally, I would get a really good lick in and feel as though I did something great, laughing and teasing whoever was on the receiving end of my slap, while the onlookers did the same. This only turned up the heat and added wrestling to the "sessions" and my excitement!

I remember one time being put in a sleeper hold until I almost passed out! One would think I had learned my lesson after this. Not so. I wanted to learn how to do it, and I did. There were times when I would jump on one of the boy's backs and wrap my right forearm around his neck, locking my right hand on my left bicep with my left hand pushing the head forward. That restricted the windpipe and could potentially crush it from the front and back, making it next to impossible to breathe. I would keep my grip locked tight until they would tap out or say "Uncle."

Whatever they did to me, I would work hard to learn how to do it to them. I never did accomplish beating any of them, but I sure did have fun and learn a lot trying. The things I learned in times like these and many others, along with the love I developed for the sport of boxing, became the foundation on which I would build my ability to defend myself.

When I got older, some of the guys would call for me when they had problems with females, and I would answer every time. I never shied away from fighting, whether male (which I fought most) or female. Fighting was a way of life for us. It was normal. It was welcomed. It was fun.

Warrior's Evolution

The love The Father shows me teaches me to seek other means of expressing myself through effective communication. Today, I understand and agree with what the Bible says:

> For we are not fighting against flesh-and-blood enemies, but against evil rulers and authorities of the unseen world, against mighty powers in this dark world, and against evil spirits in the heavenly places.
> (Ephesians 6:12 NLT)

The Word of God has taught me how to recognize the real enemy. By His grace, truth has been made manifest to me. There is an enemy we can't see using the people we can see. By keeping us focused on who we can see, the enemy continues to fly under the radar, not being exposed as the puppet master he is.

> **THERE IS AN ENEMY WE CAN'T SEE USING THE PEOPLE WE CAN SEE.**

When I was fighting my friend on that day in the courtyard, the enemy was behind it all. My growing desire to never feel inferior again was part of an elaborate scheme concocted by the enemy to take me down the path of destruction. Sadly, for a long time, it worked. That desire gave way to anger, which showed up as fighting and evolved into rage.

I remember one of the last fights I had. The fight ended with me coming to myself after having blacked out and my friend frantically yelling, "Stop Piggy, you gon' kill her!" At that moment, I recognized something was horribly wrong with me. Yet, I didn't know how to fix it. At this point in my life, I did not know the Lord. In my own strength, I worked hard not to get that angry. And I didn't. That shook me to my core.

The enemy does not care how young we are when he puts his plan into motion. I was about four years old! I believe the enemy's philosophy is "the younger, the better." The younger we are when he begins his assault, the less likely we are to recognize it's him behind the scenes pulling the strings.

This is why it's crucial that we, as parents, cover our children with the blood of Jesus and not overlook certain behaviors. Not only must we learn and practice effective communication, but we must also teach our children to do the same from a young age. We must do as the Bible admonishes us in Proverbs 22:6, "Train up a child in the way he should go..." This is utterly pivotal.

Remember how I shared that I began to build a foundation for defending myself against the violence in my early life? My behavior was not addressed nor corrected. It was mocked and then celebrated. Had the enemy continued to have his way, that very behavior would have been my final and total destruction.

But! God said not so!

The Right Fight

Today, I fight with the Word of God. I fight in prayer. I fight with fasting. I fight with faith. I fight with obedience and submission to the Word of God. I fight with the right thinking and right speaking. I fight with humility. The Father has given us so many tools with which to fight!

Where I once fought wrong, at this stage in my life, I fight right. Just as I practiced learning how to fight in the flesh, I practiced what The Father shared and revealed about fighting in the Spirit. You see, Ephesians Chapter 6 goes on to say:

> Wherefore take unto you the whole armour of God, that ye may be able to withstand in the evil day, and having done all, to stand. Stand therefore, having your loins girt about with truth, and having on the breastplate of righteousness; and your feet shod with the preparation of the gospel of peace; above all, taking the shield of faith, wherewith ye shall be able to quench all the fiery darts of the wicked. And take the helmet of salvation, and the sword of the Spirit, which is the word of God: praying always with all prayer and supplication in the Spirit, and watching thereunto with all perseverance and supplication for all saints. (Ephesians 6:13-18)

I have learned to defeat the enemy by fighting right. As long as we arm ourselves likewise and put on the whole armor of God, we can't lose! No matter how it started, there is room to make lasting changes. No matter how it's going, there's room to make adjustments. No matter what the enemy has said, the end will be, you must keep fighting. Your very survival depends on it.

Why? Because if you look closely at Ephesians 6:18 you will see that the armor isn't just about the one wearing it. The armor is also for our brothers and sisters in Christ. They are saints. Our fight is bigger than us. Our fight is for more than just us. Our fight is not just about us.

Keep Fighting

My fight was for you. I had to continue to fight (the right way) so I could write these words of encouragement to you. Had I quit fighting, how could I have encouraged you to continue? I ask you the same questions: How can you encourage someone else to continue if you quit fighting?

It's tough, but keep fighting. It hurts, but keep fighting. It may even look like you're losing, but keep fighting. Fight until you see change. Fight until you see the transformation. Fight until your joy is replenished. Fight until your strength is renewed. Fight until your peace is restored. Fight until your faith comes alive. Fight!

> **FIGHT UNTIL YOU SEE THE TRANSFORMATION.**

Fight until the enemy backs off, and when he comes back again, fight some more. Scripture teaches us:

> Submit yourselves therefore to God. Resist the devil, and he will flee from you. (James 4:7)

When we fight right, in the Spirit and not in the flesh, we demonstrate resistance and the ability to withstand the onslaught of the enemy. When we validate our endurance by our resistance, the Bible assures us that the enemy WILL flee from us; he will make a hasty retreat, and God will turn things around in our favor. I'm reminded of this proclamation in the Word:

> And we know [with great confidence] that God [who is deeply concerned about us] causes all things to work together [as a plan] for good for those who love God, to those who are called according to His plan and purpose. (Romans 8:28 AMP)

Our Father causes all things, all situations, all circumstances, all mess-ups, all mix-ups, all hang-ups, etc., to work on our behalf. When I yielded to Christ, I didn't stop fighting. I just learned how to fight the right way. My hands, feet, and mouth are now surrendered to the Lord for Him to use as He desires.

I told, and continue to tell, the enemy "I am no longer available for use by you." This is one of the ways I continue to fight and resist the enemy. I refuse to be a tool in the enemy's tool shed. I refuse to be the one the enemy uses to destroy my brother or sister. I refuse to be a slave to unrighteousness. I choose to fight right.

Our battle is in the spiritual realm, this is where God has given us authority. After fighting in the flesh and failing time and again, something clicked. I finally grasped what The Father was telling me in 1 Corinthians 10:4 that the weapons of our warfare are not carnal. I had been fighting spiritual battles in the flesh. That is why I wasn't seeing victory. Oh, but when I started fighting in the spirit, I experienced victory like I had never experienced before! You, too, can experience victory!

What are some of the ways you fight?

What weapons do you use?

Are you fighting spiritual battles in the flesh?

How can you improve the way you fight?

> **A Little Girl's Recommendation:** Teach me what it means to fight right? Teach me how to resolve conflict. Teach me what it means to forgive and how to apologize and mean it.

My Prayer for Little Girls

Father, I pray You reveal the spiritual weapons to little girls that You have equipped them with. I pray You show them in dreams and visions how and when to use those weapons to defend themselves against the attacks of the enemy. I pray You give them an unusual mental and spiritual toughness against the forces of darkness. I pray You reveal the significance of the armor to them. I pray You supernaturally reveal the function of each piece of armor. I pray for the strength of little girls when it's time to stand. I pray they stand sure and unwavering. I pray they stand firm and unshakeable. I pray they stand fortified and resolute in You and in Your Word. In Jesus' name. Amen.

Chapter 8
YOU. SHALL. OVERCOME!

In every corner of our lives, from personal struggles to broader societal issues, the assurance of overcoming adversity is a central theme in Scripture. This life is woven with threads of trials and triumphs, and despite Satan's plan, the promise of overcoming adversity stands as a beacon of hope.

The "You shall overcome" promise is not a vague hope or mere comforting platitude but a powerful, biblically grounded truth and scriptural reality underscoring the strength and victory promised to believers. The Father wants to challenge your rationale and shift your perspective. If you would lend your hearts to what He is speaking, You. Shall. Overcome!

Overcome. Vanquish. Conquer. Crush. Defeat. Overpower. Subdue. Prevail. Each of these words describes what the enemy planned to do to you. He wanted to destroy you with what happened to you. He wanted to crush you with what they did to you. He wanted to conquer you by any means necessary. Think back on some of the things you have experienced in life and examine how you responded to them. Did you respond according to the Word of God, or did you respond according to the dictates of the enemy?

If you responded according to the dictates of the enemy, he won in those moments. I have responded both ways. Our maturity in the things of God lessens the times when we respond as the enemy would have us to. We mature in God by frequenting Him, His presence, His Word.

You see, the goal of the enemy is to win situation by situation until he gets us to a place of despair and hopelessness where we decide to give up on trying altogether. When we get to that place, he can work on us all the more to get us to deny the way of the Lord for good. That serpent of old wraps himself around us as a python would its prey and squeezes tighter and tighter until we give up, throw in the towel and denounce Jesus Christ.

Some of us feel that way right now as if the enemy is squeezing us. And he very well might be! However, we must stay in faith and continue to contend for the victory God has promised us in His Word! No matter how tight the enemy squeezes, no matter how tight his grip may seem, no matter how tough things get, no matter how muddy the waters, no matter how dark the road, we must remember and declare, encouraging ourselves in the Lord, "IN THE END, I WIN! VICTORY IS MINE!"

Faith's Furnace

A key verse for understanding our victory over trials is found in 1 John:

> For everyone born of God overcomes the world. This is the victory that has overcome the world, even our faith. (1 John 5:4)

This verse clearly outlines that overcoming the world is inherently linked to our faith in Christ. It is through our relationship with Jesus that we gain the power to conquer life's challenges. Paul echoes this victorious theme:

> No, in all these things we are more than conquerors through him who loved us. (Romans 8:37 NIV)

This passage follows a powerful discussion on the sufferings of the present time and the assurance that nothing can separate us from the love of God. The phrase "more than conquerors" implies a victory that surpasses mere survival or endurance—it's a triumphant, abundant victory through Christ's love.

Just days before encountering Christ's love for me (and seven some days after) when it felt like my very breath was being taken from me. Like the oxygen in my lungs was being sucked out of me. Like life was being choked out of me. I was suffocating. In a zombie-like state. Catatonic, if you will. Going through the motions and routine of everyday, mundane life. Defeated. No will. No drive. No desire. No ambition. A dead woman walking. I was deteriorating.

Alternate Reality

Outwardly, a different portrait was painted. I had learned to be the best craftsman, meticulously stroking the canvas of my life as I wanted the world to see it. Some days, I would skillfully sketch strength, toughness, and stability. Other days, I would sketch courage, certainty, and mental and physical toughness. Visibly, I would be chipper and upbeat. I would engage others in conversation, appearing present while simultaneously hiding the truth that my mind was light-years away.

It became easier and easier for me to mask the real me. Inwardly, I lacked confidence, was unsure of myself, and was self-deprecating; I hid behind others' compliments of me. "You're so strong." "You always seem so sure of yourself." "I wish I could be as confident as you." I lived based on others' perspectives of me and shunned the truth I knew about myself. I completely and utterly ignored my inadequacies, refusing to address the issues that leisurely feasted on my inner self.

I permitted others' outlook of me to become my escape mechanism. If they saw me in a positive light, there was no need for me to see myself the way I was. I had become skilled in dealing with the difficulties of my reality by camouflaging my reality with others' opinions of me. I lived in their opinions. I resided in an alternate reality.

> **I PERMITTED OTHERS' OUTLOOK OF ME TO BECOME MY ESCAPE MECHANISM.**

In this alternate place, I was fun, loving, and outgoing. The life of the party. I lived like there was no tomorrow. No regard for my life. After all, it wasn't worth much. So, I lived recklessly. Yet when the lights went out, reality set in. I was as equally dark on the inside as the atmosphere on the outside. Because of my coping skills, I had lost touch with reality. I lived as though the alternate reality was my actual reality for so long that that's what it became. I lived like that for years. I lost myself. I lost my identity. The enemy had me.

Have you ever been there? Have you ever been in a place where what others thought of you was more desirable than what *you* thought about yourself? There were never conversations about what was slowly eating away at me inside. This further exacerbated the situation.

For years, the sexual violations, the abandonment, the rejection, the low self-esteem, the low sense of self-worth, and the desire to be loved slowly and strategically gnawed away at me. Devouring me little by little, piece by piece, bit by bit. Eventually, what I thought had been inconspicuous became crystal clear. I had come face to face, nose to nose, eyeball to eyeball with the hardest truth. I was pinned down, held captive, and imprisoned by the experiences of my past.

The Past Had Passed

My frame of mind was exactly what the enemy banked on. Why? Because he knows that when we allow the complexities of our past to become our present, they hinder our future. Day after day, we drag the past with us, refusing to detach, disassociate, and disunite with it. We refuse to divorce it!

For some of us, letting go of the past means confronting and exposing what we have kept hidden for so long. For others, letting go of the past means we must do battle and contend with the lies of the enemy. The truth is, some of us have held on to the past for so long that we don't know who we are apart from it. So, leaving it seems more scary than being free from it.

Can I let you in on a little secret? The past has passed. The only place the past is present is in your mind. This is why renewing our minds by the Word of God is so crucial. The Bible directs us in the book of Romans.

> Let God transform you into a new person by changing the way you think. (Romans 12:2a NLT)

The enemy does not want you to come into the knowledge that by God's faultless and unfailing grace, you overcame what was trying to overcome you! The fact that you're reading this book is a testimony to the fact that you have OVERCOME. The fact that you are alive gives evidence to the truth that you have OVERCOME. The fact that you are still in your right mind bears witness to the truth that you have OVERCOME. You have already survived what the enemy hoped you would succumb to. You have already persisted, withstood, and endured. You have already OVERCOME. You made it through it.

The Power of Testimony

Be inspired and empowered by the Word of God:

> And they overcame and conquered him because of the blood of the Lamb and because of the word of their testimony, for they did not love their life and renounce their faith even when faced with death.
> (Revelation 12:11 AMP)

We declare and believe that we have overcome by the blood of the lamb. We sing about the blood. We shout about the blood. We dance about the blood. At times, we even plead the blood! But we seem to have overlooked the part about "the words of our testimony." WHAT WE SAY IS IMPORTANT!

The words we speak are a sign of agreement with whoever the source of those words is. When we speak the Word of God, we signify that we agree with Him. Similarly, when we speak the words of Satan, we make it evident that we agree with him. So, the question becomes, "What are you saying about your past?"

> **WHAT ARE YOU SAYING ABOUT YOUR PAST?**

Proverbs 18:21 tells us that the power of life and death is in the tongue. We have the power and authority to give life or death to whatever and whoever we are speaking about. Could it be that your past is still present because you constantly and consistently furnish the power necessary for it to live by what you continue to say? Think about that. Every word we speak is either giving life to something or killing something. We have the power in our mouths to control whether or not the past continues to live. You do. I do. We do. Know and recognize the weight of your voice.

Divine Muscle

The Father has given us power. However, although He has given us the power to overcome, we must realize that our ability to overcome is not rooted in our strength but in our reliance on God and His Word. By relying on Him, having confidence in what the blood of the Lamb provided us, sharing our testimonies, and standing firm in faith, we embody the victory promised in Revelation 12:11. When reliance on God is the posture of our hearts, we can face and overcome any challenge through prayer, perseverance, and the assurance of God's presence.

The notion of overcoming is closely tied to perseverance and hope. The scriptures lovingly declare:

> Blessed is the one who perseveres under trial because, having stood the test, that person will receive the crown of life that the Lord has promised to those who love him. (James 1:12 NIV)

This verse illustrates that perseverance through trials leads to divine rewards, emphasizing that overcoming is a process that leads to spiritual growth and ultimate blessings. Additionally, Apostle Paul offers further encouragement:

> I pray that God, the source of hope, will fill you completely with joy and peace because you trust in him. Then, you will overflow with confident hope through the power of the Holy Spirit. (Romans 15:13 NLT)

This verse underscores the role of hope in our journey. It is through trusting in God that we are filled with joy, peace, and an overflowing hope that empowers us to overcome.

We have an excellent and the ultimate example of overcoming in Jesus Christ Himself!

> We do this by keeping our eyes on Jesus, the champion who initiates and perfects our faith. Because of the joy awaiting him, he endured the cross, disregarding its shame. Now he is seated in the place of honor beside God's throne. (Hebrews 12:2 NLT)

Drawing strength and inspiration from His example, Christ's endurance and victory over suffering and death are the ultimate assurance that we, too, shall overcome.

A Little Girl's Recommendation: Teach me not to be a mean girl or a bully. Teach me how beautiful I am inside and out. Teach me that I am victorious through Jesus Christ.

My Prayer for Little Girls

Father, when faced with situations that are too difficult for their minds to understand, assure little girls of their victory through Your Son, Jesus Christ. Even teach them that natural victory is good but eternal victory is what they should strive for. Father, reveal to them that Jesus Christ is the victory that has overcome the world. Teach them they can do all things through Christ. Father, let them know that true strength is found only in Christ and in Your Word. Keep them from false religion. Keep them from false teachers. Keep them from false christs. Keep them from wolves in sheep's clothing. Keep them as the apple of your eye and hide them under the shadow of your wings. Let them know that You are their safe space and the name of Jesus is their safe word. In Jesus' name. Amen.

Chapter 9
THE POWER OF FORGIVENESS

Forgiveness was the key to unlocking the door leading to better. It is the act of letting go of resentment, anger, or the desire for revenge towards someone who has caused you harm or wrongdoing. It involves releasing negative emotions and choosing to move forward without holding the offense against the person who committed it.

For many, this is the toughest part of the journey to overcoming. It's so easy to hold on to resentment, anger, and desire for revenge. But why do we rationalize unforgiveness? "They did what they did. They said what they said. They made me feel how they made me feel. I have a right to feel the way I feel!" That was me—rationalizing unforgiveness, justifying my emotions, holding on to unrighteous indignation, wearing the past as part of my day-to-day wardrobe like it was a fashion statement!

Unforgiveness, bitterness, anger, strife, malice, frustration, mercilessness, resentment, spite—these were my undergarments. All of these were holding me together. They were my support. They were my crutch. They were my leaning post.

One day, the Lord spoke something so profound to me, "The blood was for them too!" I was floored! Speechless! I hadn't even considered that the blood Jesus shed was for them, too. I was so blinded by the "They did what they did… I have a right to feel the way I feel" part of me that I failed to realize that the cross was for them, too. This was a sobering reality. The enemy had me so engrossed in what happened to me that I overlooked the love of God for them.

> **THE BLOOD WAS FOR THEM TOO!**

In my error, I reasoned that there was no room for God to love a person like them. Have you had the same thoughts? I atoned myself with the lies of the enemy. How arrogant I was! How could I assume that the things I had done to others weren't disqualifiers of The Father's love for me but what was done to me disqualified them from God loving them? Have you ever felt like that? Do you see the hypocrisy of that?

Quicksand

When The Father spoke this in my spirit, it hit me like a ton of bricks. He tenderly reminded me that if I wanted to be forgiven I had to forgive. Almost immediately after The Lord spoke this, the enemy came with every reason imaginable why they didn't deserve my forgiveness. The enemy wanted me to stay in the place of "Max, you deserve forgiveness but they don't. What you did to others wasn't as bad as what they did to you."

This is where many of us remain stuck. Right here. Right in this place of comparison; comparing sins to determine which ones are pardonable and which ones should be punished to the fullest extent of the law. This is a trick of the enemy. The place of comparison is quicksand! Don't allow the enemy to deceive you into believing that this line of reasoning is ok.

When someone steps into quicksand, they often become more deeply ensnared the more they try to move, as the sand's suction increases with movement. Once trapped, movement becomes difficult, leading to a state of inertia. Being trapped in quicksand requires significant effort to escape, draining physical energy and causing panic. I was trapped in the quicksand of comparison! The more I compared, the deeper the trap, the more I was being sucked into self.

A Spoonful of Sugar

None of us were worthy of the blood shed of Jesus Christ. None of us! The Father wasn't in Heaven comparing sins to determine which ones He would send His Son for. He sent His Son to die for sins once and for all (1 Peter 3:18 AMP). Christ died for them too. He died for the one who violated you. He died for the one who lied on you. He died for the one who abandoned you. He died for the one who abused you mentally, physically, and emotionally. Whatever they did to you, He died for them, too.

That was a hard pill to swallow. I needed Mary Poppins' spoonful of sugar to make this medicine go down. I had been confronted with the truth, and that truth demanded a decision: Yield to the Word and forgive. Can I be honest, though? This yielding wasn't as easy as it sounds. In fact, it was most difficult and draining. I didn't want to forgive. I was solid in my stance that forgiveness for what was done to me wasn't deserved, especially since I received no apology!

I kicked & screamed. I fought & questioned. I reasoned & rehearsed! I cried until my eyes were red and swollen, more than once! But, I knew the Word of God was right. So, although I didn't want to, I forgave. My obedience to God and my desire to do His will led me to forgive.

We will not overcome without first forgiving. In comparison, unforgiveness is like quicksand. Unforgiveness traps, immobilizes, and drains those who hold onto it. Just as escaping quicksand requires specific actions and often external help, moving past unforgiveness requires a conscious decision to forgive, realizing the blood was for them, seeking support, and taking steps towards emotional and spiritual healing by the Word of God.

The Process of Forgiveness

Forgiveness is not about excusing others' behavior or forgetting what happened. It's about freeing yourself from the burden of bitterness and allowing God's healing to take place in your heart. It's a process, often a painful one, but it's necessary for true healing and growth.

The scripture reminds us in Ephesians 4:32, "Be kind and compassionate to one another, forgiving each other, just as in Christ God forgave you." This verse became a cornerstone in my journey of forgiveness.

As I wrestled with forgiveness, I found myself returning to Matthew 18:21-22, where Peter asks Jesus, "Lord, how many times shall I forgive my brother or sister who sins against me? Up to seven times?" Jesus answered, "I tell you, not seven times, but seventy-seven times." This passage challenged me to see forgiveness not as a one-time event but as an ongoing process, a way of life.

I began to realize that forgiveness is a choice we make, sometimes daily, sometimes moment by moment. It's not about waiting for feelings to change but about making a decision to release the offender from the debt they owe us, even when every emotion in our body screams for justice.

The journey of forgiveness often feels like two steps forward and one step back. There were days when I thought I had forgiven, only to find anger and resentment resurface unexpectedly. In those moments, I had to choose forgiveness all over again. It was in this repeated choosing that I found my heart slowly changing, the bitterness gradually giving way to compassion.

The Ripple Effect

As I embraced forgiveness, I discovered a new chapter of my life unfolding—one filled with purpose and transformation. The weight I had been carrying for so long began to lift, and I could finally breathe freely. The process of forgiving others opened the door for me to forgive myself as well, which was equally important in my healing journey.

I didn't expect how forgiveness would impact *every* area of my life. My relationships improved as I became less defensive and more open. My mental health flourished as I released the toxic thoughts that had been plaguing me. Even my physical health seemed to benefit as the stress of holding onto grudges melted away.

I found myself able to empathize more with others, recognizing that everyone is fighting their own battles. This newfound empathy allowed me to connect with people on a deeper level, fostering more meaningful relationships.

Forgiveness doesn't mean reconciliation in all cases, although reconciliation is the objective of forgiveness. Sometimes, forgiving means loving someone from a distance. It means choosing peace for yourself, regardless of whether the other person ever acknowledges their wrongdoing or seeks your forgiveness. This was a crucial lesson for me—understanding that I could forgive someone without allowing them a seat on the front row of my life if their presence was harmful.

The Freedom of Forgiveness

As I continued on this path of forgiveness, I experienced a freedom I had never known before. The chains of bitterness and resentment that had bound me for so long began to fall away. I found myself able to think about past hurts without being overwhelmed by negative emotions. The power those memories possessed over me diminished.

> **THE POWER THOSE MEMORIES POSSESSED OVER ME DIMINISHED.**

This freedom allowed me to redirect my energy towards positive pursuits. Instead of constantly replaying old hurts, I could focus on personal growth, nurturing healthy relationships, and pursuing God's purposes for my life. I discovered talents and passions that had been buried under layers of pain and anger.

> And we know that God causes everything to work together for the good of those who love God and are called according to his purpose for them.
>
> (Romans 8:28 NLT)

Moreover, forgiveness opened my eyes to see the hand of God even in my difficult experiences. I learned how to give God glory even during the darkest times. I began to understand how He could use all things—even the painful ones—for good, as Romans 8:28 promises. This didn't mean that what happened to me was good, but that God, in His infinite wisdom and love, could bring good out of it.

Remember, forgiveness is a choice, not a feeling. You may not feel like forgiving, but you can choose to forgive. And as you make that choice repeatedly, your feelings will eventually catch up with your decision. Colossians instructs us:

> Bear with each other and forgive one another if any of you has a grievance against someone. Forgive as the Lord forgave you. (Colossians 3:13)

Forgiveness is not weakness; it's strength. It takes courage to forgive, to let go of what you think you deserve, and to choose a different path. But in that courage, in that choice, lies true freedom and the power to break cycles of hurt and pain.

> **A Little Girl's Recommendation:** Teach me about forgiveness early. Show me how to forgive through your actions. Help me understand that forgiveness is for my benefit, not just for others.

My Prayer for Little Girls

Heavenly Father, I pray for the little girls who are struggling with forgiveness. Give them the strength and wisdom to understand the power of forgiveness. Help them see that forgiving doesn't mean forgetting, but it means releasing the pain and hurt to You. Teach them that forgiveness is a gift they give themselves. Guide them to forgive not only others but also themselves. Surround them with people who model forgiveness in their own lives. Let them experience the freedom and peace that comes with forgiveness. In Jesus' name, Amen.

Chapter 10
EMERGING VICTORIOUS

With forgiveness as my foundation, I began to see the fruits of my journey in every aspect of my life. The process of forgiveness led me to a place of repentance—a turning away from old thought patterns and behaviors that had kept me bound.

Once I yielded to the truth, I repented for believing, agreeing with, and holding on to the lies of the enemy. I repented for allowing the enemy to use me as a storehouse for his works. I repented for allowing the enemy to use me to do his bidding. Repentance was necessary. Without repentance, I wouldn't be reconciled to the truth.

The more I leaned into truth, the more I could feel the liberating power of truth at work in me. The truth was freeing me! Truth was chipping away at that wall I built. Truth was tearing down the idol I made of my past. Truth was stripping me of unrighteousness and building me up in Christ Jesus simultaneously. Truth was pulling me up and out of the quicksand of comparison and unforgiveness.

Cocoon Chronicles

I liken my journey to that of a butterfly coming out of its cocoon after the process of metamorphosis. Before the butterfly was a butterfly, it was a caterpillar. The caterpillar had everything inside of it to become what it was intended to be, but it had to go through a process. Without the process, the caterpillar doesn't reach its full potential. Without the process, the caterpillar doesn't become what God created and intended it to be. Without going through its process, the caterpillar can't go as far, reach as many, or influence as much.

We all have processes to go and grow through. We go in one way, and after some time, after some changes, after some shifting, we come out a brand new and beautiful creation.

This metamorphosis wasn't just a physical or emotional change but a spiritual transformation. As I allowed God to work in me, I found myself developing new perspectives, new habits, and a new identity rooted in Christ rather than in my past experiences.

My journey to overcoming wasn't easy. It wasn't pretty—in fact, at times, it was downright ugly—but it was worth it. It started out rocky, with some twists and turns. The water was muddy and murky. But along the way, I learned some things. I learned some things about myself. I learned some things about Christ, some things about The Father, how to lean on The Lord, and how to trust Him.

I have forgiven and have been forgiven. It wasn't until I forgave that my life began to change for the better from the inside out. That's how He changes us. The Lord has taken out that old, stony, calloused, nasty, hateful, bitter heart and has given me a new heart. A heart that forgives and loves; a caring and compassionate heart. He has given me His heart.

> **HE HAS GIVEN ME HIS HEART.**

I decided not to allow my past to control me anymore. I chose who and what I wanted to bow to. I chose to bow to no one except the True and Living God and His Word. This decision was a turning point in my life. It marked the moment when I truly began to live in victory rather than as a victim.

Emerging victorious doesn't mean that life becomes perfect or that challenges disappear. It means that we face life's difficulties with a new strength, a new perspective, and a new identity. It means that we no longer allow our past to dictate our future. Instead, we use our experiences as stepping stones to a greater purpose.

As I reflect on my journey, a poem I wrote years ago takes on new meaning:

All Grown Up I Vaguely Understand

Copyright © 2008 Maxine Jackson

All grown up, I vaguely understand
Why daddy had to kill that man
For having his hand in the cookie jar.
Too young to comprehend
The ugliness of the situation
And the determination of that man
To conquer the girl
So young and innocent
Yet, ignorant
To the wrong which was being done
She failed to say a word.
Out of shame, fear, and blame
Afraid of judgment and disbelief
To be placed upon her name.
So instead, this indiscretion lay hid
In the tiniest corner of the heart
Until on that day,
That man was caught.
All grown up, I vaguely understand.

This poem captures the confusion and pain of my younger self. Just for the record, Daddy didn't kill anybody. That was just an expression. Now, with the perspective of time and healing, I understand that while we may never fully comprehend the actions of others, we can choose to move forward in forgiveness and strength. Our experiences, even the painful ones, can become the very things that God uses to shape us and prepare us for our purpose.

EMERGING VICTORIOUS

So, I speak to the little girl in you and encourage her to speak up and out. Free yourself by exposing the works of the enemy. Write down your experiences. Share them with a trusted friend or family member. Make an appointment with your Pastor or First Lady. Go into your prayer closet and tell The Lord about it. Just get it out of you. There's more room on the outside than there is on the inside. Love yourself enough to want to be free from the grip of your past experiences. Open your mouth and say something! Freedom awaits you.

> **A Little Girl's Recommendation:** Show me how to be strong and brave. Teach me that my past doesn't define my future. Help me understand that I can use my experiences to help others.

My Prayer for Little Girls

Heavenly Father, I lift up every little girl who is on the journey to overcoming. Give them the courage to face their fears and the strength to persevere through challenges. Help them to see themselves as You see them—precious, valuable, and full of potential. Surround them with people who will encourage them and speak life into their situations. Let them know that their voice matters and that their experiences can be used for good. Guide them to discover their purpose and to walk in it confidently. May they emerge victorious, not just for themselves, but as beacons of hope for others. In Jesus' name, Amen.

Conclusion

This journey has taught me so much and exposed me to love as I had never known it. Today, I love myself. I had to love myself enough not to allow what others did to me to be a barrier to where my soul would spend eternity. Today, I love The Father, and I am certain He loves me. He has been the glue holding me together all these years.

Today, I have been married for almost a decade! My sons have had the privilege of witnessing my transformation. They have witnessed my caterpillar state and my cocoon state. Now, they are witnessing my butterfly state.

At this stage in life, I have been able to go further than I ever dreamed I would. I was the first in my family to graduate from college. I have a thriving career in accounting. I am a licensed Evangelist in the Lord's church. But most importantly, I have allowed and continue to allow the Word of God to be the driving force behind all I do.

My story is a testament to the transformative power of God's love and the strength that comes from choosing to overcome. It's proof that our past does not have to dictate our future and that with God, all things are truly possible.

I pray your eyes have been opened to guidance and a fresh perspective. I hope you've been empowered and inspired by this portion of my story. May you have found renewed strength, hope, and peace and risen above your pain. I trust that through my journey, your faith has been increased.

The Following Resources

But our journey doesn't end here. In the following appendices, you'll find additional resources to support your continued growth. These tools are designed to aid you on your path of recovery, transformation, and divine strength. Remember, overcoming is your portion. Overcomer is who you are. Having overcome is your destiny.

As you explore these resources, may they teach you how to respect yourself, cultivate great manners, and show human kindness. Your story is still unfolding, and I am certain that with these tools and God's grace, you shall overcome.

To all the little girls out there and the little girl inside every woman reading this: You are strong. You are brave. You are loved. Your voice matters. Your experiences, even the painful ones, can be used for good. Don't let anyone or anything dim your light. You have a purpose, and the world needs your unique gifts.

To be continued... in your beautiful journey of healing and growth. Remember, you shall overcome!

Appendix A
KINGDOM TOOLBOX

*L*isten up, warrior! You're not just healing; you're rising. This toolbox? It's not just a collection of tips—it's your war chest, filled with God-breathed strategies to help you reclaim your crown. We're talking about weapons of spiritual warfare, divine instruments of transformation that'll have the enemy shaking in his boots.

In these pages, you'll find tools sharper than any two-edged sword, ready to cut through the lies that have held you captive. We've got prayers that'll set your spirit on fire, Scripture that'll rewire your mind, and prophetic declarations that'll make the mountains in your life tremble.

Remember, your healing isn't just about you feeling better—it's about you stepping into the fullness of who God created you to be. It's about you walking in authority, dripping in the anointing that comes from knowing Whose you are.

So go ahead, dive in. Try these tools on for size. Mix and match them like the queen you are. And watch as God turns your mess into your message, your pain into your purpose.

It's time to rise up, shake off the dust, and reclaim your royal identity. Let's get to work, shall we? Your breakthrough is waiting.

Scripture Slaying

It's time to arm yourself with the Word. When those doubts come creeping in, hit them with the truth:

> I am more than a conqueror through Him who loved me.
> (Romans 8:37)

> No weapon formed against me shall prosper.
> (Isaiah 54:17)

> I can do all things through Christ who strengthens me.
> (Philippians 4:13)

Write these down, stick them on your mirror, and make them your phone background. Let the Word be the first thing you see and the last thing you say.

Holy Ghost Hype Sessions

Sometimes, you need to be your own cheerleader. Try these Spirit-filled affirmations:

> "I am chosen, royal, and set apart for God's purpose."

> "My past is redeemed, my present is purposeful, my future is promised."

> "I walk in divine favor and supernatural blessing."

Speak these out loud, with authority. Remember, you're not just talking to yourself—you're reminding the enemy Who you belong to.

Warfare Journaling

Time to spill that tea on paper, sis. But we're not just venting—we're strategizing:

> "What lie is the enemy trying to sell me today, and what's God's truth about it?"

> "Where do I need to extend forgiveness, including to myself?"

> "What giant in my life needs to come down, and what's my 'David strategy' to defeat it?"

Praise Break Practices

When the pressure's on, it's time to turn up the praise. Create a playlist of worship songs that speak to your spirit. Dance, shout, lift those hands—let your praise become your weapon.

Kingdom Meditation

Fill your mind and your space with the things of The Lord. Soak in God's presence:

> Find a quiet spot and turn on some instrumental worship.

> Take deep breaths, inviting the Holy Spirit to fill you.

> Visualize yourself seated with Christ in heavenly places (Ephesians 2:6).

> Let His peace wash over you like a river.

Prophetic Declarations

It's time to speak life into your situation. God framed the world with His words, and you're made in His image.

> "Strongholds of fear and doubt, I demolish you in Jesus' name!"

> "Doors of opportunity and favor, you are opening for me right now!"

> "My past no longer defines me. I am who God says I am!"

Speak these with fire, with faith, with the authority of a daughter of the King!

Gratitude Glam

Thankfulness isn't just polite; it's powerful. Start and end your day by listing three things you're grateful for. Watch how it shifts your perspective from victim to victor.

Spiritual Squad Goals

Surround yourself with faith-filled friends who'll pray with you, prophesy over you, and push you into your purpose. Iron sharpens iron, sis!

Fasting for Breakthrough

Sometimes, you have to shut down the natural to tune into the supernatural. Try fasting from food, social media, or anything louder than God's voice in your life.

Serve it Up

Nothing breaks chains like helping others break theirs. Find a ministry, mentor someone, or volunteer. Your testimony is someone else's lifeline.

Holy Ghost Fitness

Your body is a temple, so let's get it in shape for God's glory! Exercise, eat well, and rest. A healthy body fuels a focused mind and a strong soul.

Bedtime Blessings

Before you sleep, speak blessings over your life, your home, and your future. Let the last words on your lips be faith-filled declarations.

Remember, champion, these tools aren't just exercises—they're exchanges. They aren't just accessories—they're necessities for the woman of God who's ready to level up. They're your secret weapons in a world that's trying to keep you small. Every time you use one of these tools, you're trading your weakness for His strength, your brokenness for His wholeness.

Appendix B
YOUR GLOW-UP GUIDE

*L*isten up, family! This isn't just a journey; it's your royal procession. You are going to strut into your destiny. These are steps to slay in your God-given purpose:

Throne Room Check-Ins
Schedule daily audiences with the King of Kings. This may not be "quiet time." Get loud, get real, get transformed.

Slay Your Giants
Read 1 Samuel 17 and identify those Goliaths in your life, whether they're fear, addiction, or doubt. It's time to take them down, David-style.

Kingdom Creativity
Unleash that God-given imagination! Write, sing, dance, create. Let your art become your warfare.

Destiny Detox
It's time to cleanse. What habits, relationships, or thoughts are holding you back? Let's flush them out.

Purpose-Driven Glow-Up
Align your life with your calling. Make your career, relationships, and everything else serve your God-given purpose.

Holy Ghost Glow

Cultivate that inner radiance. Let the joy of the Lord be your strength and your beauty secret.

Legacy Building

Think beyond yourself. How are you impacting generations to come? Start laying those foundation stones now.

Remember, this journey isn't just about healing. It's about revealing the masterpiece God always intended you to be. So, beautiful, brave, blessed child of God, it's time to work your toolbox like your destiny depends on it—because it does. Now, go out there and show them what a woman looks like when she's fully alive in her purpose, walking in her anointing, and unstoppable in her faith! Your breakthrough isn't just coming—it's chasing you down. All you have to do is turn around and embrace it. Let's go!

Appendix C
RESOURCES

The Holy Bible (reader's choice of translation) is my primary resource in life, guiding my decisions, values, and understanding of the world. Its timeless wisdom and teachings serve as a compass for navigating life's challenges and celebrating its joys.

Books

The following books cover a range of topics, including healing from past trauma, establishing healthy boundaries, understanding one's worth in Christ, emotional healing, and spiritual growth. They can provide valuable insights and practical strategies for those continuing their journey of healing and overcoming.

Allender, Dan B. *The Wounded Heart: Hope for Adult Victims of Childhood Sexual Abuse*. NavPress, 2008.

Edgecombe, Tiffany. *A Time to Heal: Restoration from the Ravages of Rape*. Christian Living Books, Inc., 2021.

—. *Overcoming Obstacles: A Fight to the Finish*. Christian Living Books, Inc., 2016.

Jakes, T. D. *Woman Thou Art Loosed*. Destiny Image Publishers, 2007.

—. *Crushing: God Turns Pressure into Power.* FaithWords, 2018.

Kemp, Vicki. *Better than Yesterday: Proverbs of a Woman's Heart.* Christian Living Books, Inc., 2018.

—. *Grace in Deep Waters.* Christian Living Books, Inc., 2021.

King, Clayton. *Overcome: Replacing the Lies That Hold Us Down with the Truths That Set Us Free.* Baker Books, 2015.

Meyer, Joyce. *Battlefield of the Mind: Winning the Battle in Your Mind.* FaithWords, 2002.

Omartian, Stormie. *The Power of a Praying Woman.* Harvest House Publishers, 2014.

Phillips, Dr. Anita. *The Garden Within: Where the War with Your Emotions Ends and Your Most Powerful Life Begins.* Thomas Nelson, 2023.

Scazzero, Peter. *Emotionally Healthy Spirituality: It's Impossible to Be Spiritually Mature, While Remaining Emotionally Immature.* Zondervan, 2017.

Shirer, Priscilla. *Fervent: A Woman's Battle Plan to Serious, Specific, and Strategic Prayer.* B&H Books, 2015.

TerKeurst, Lysa. *Forgiving What You Can't Forget: Discover How to Move On, Make Peace with Painful Memories, and Create a Life That's Beautiful Again.* Thomas Nelson, 2020.

Van der Kolk, Bessel. *The Body Keeps the Score: Brain, Mind, and Body in the Healing of Trauma.* Viking, 2014.

Support Groups:

- Abuse Recovery Ministry Services (abuserecovery.org)
- Adult Survivors of Child Abuse (ascasupport.org)
- Celebrate Recovery (celebraterecovery.com)

Counseling Services

- BetterHelp Online Counseling (betterhelp.com)
- Christian Care Connect (christiancareconnect.com)
- Christian Counselors Network (christiancounselorsnetwork.com)
- National Domestic Abuse Hotline: 1-800-799-SAFE (7233)
- National Sexual Assault Hotline: 1-800-656-HOPE (4673)
- Suicide Prevention Lifeline: Call or text 988

If you are experiencing a mental health emergency, please call 911 immediately.

Acknowledgments

Writing a book about overcoming challenges is as much a journey as it is a personal endeavor. As I reflect on the path that led to the creation of this work, I am deeply aware that it would not have been possible without the support, encouragement, and wisdom of many remarkable individuals.

First and foremost, I want to thank God for the work He has done and continues to do in and through me. Father, I thank You for Your Son Jesus Christ, by whose bloodshed that both my overcoming and this book is possible. Thank You, Father, for rescuing me and transforming my heart. I love You with everything I am.

To my husband, Roger Henry, Jr., whose unwavering belief in me has been a constant source of strength. Honey, your support and encouragement have been a beacon during the darkest times, and your faith in my vision kept me moving forward. Thank you for staying up at night with me while I typed. Thank you for wiping away my tears when I cried. Thank you for listening when I needed an ear. Thank you for being my covering. Thank you for loving me the way you do. Thank you for being the man that you are. I thank God for you. I love you beyond what words can express.

To my son, DeAndre, my firstborn. Your arrival single-handedly changed the course of my life! When I found out I was pregnant with you at the age of 16, I needed and desired to be loved. I knew that no matter what happened, you would love me. When I held you, for the first time in my life, I felt I finally did something right. Thank you for your love and support. I admire the man you have grown to be and the determination you have to remain a fixture in the lives of your children. You are an amazing husband and father. I'm looking forward to the next chapter of your life. I love you son.

To my son, Tyrique, my conversationalist. You were always so inquisitive, seeking to understand the "why." I knew, from the moment you were able to talk, that you were going to go into a field where communicating was the cornerstone of the profession. Today, you are on the path to greatness, pursuing the highest level of education in Psychology. I am so proud of you, and I cherish every conversation. Thank you for being you. Thank you for your love and support. You are going to be an awesome husband and father. I love you son.

To my son, Jeremiah, my encourager. You are always so positive and encouraging; I love that about you. Thank you for every time you encouraged me when things were overwhelming. Thank you for always telling me how great of a job I was doing as a mom. Thank you for recognizing when I was having a hard day or tough time and hugging me, telling me it was going to be ok and that God had me. Those times will forever remain with me. Thank you, son. You, too, are going to make a wonderful husband and father. I love you son.

To my Grammie, Essie Maxine. I wish you were here. I love and miss you so much. I wish I could hug you one more time. I miss our late nights in the front yard and coming by in the wee hours of the morning, sitting with you as you water the lawn. Life without you has been tough, but God has sent me some amazing people. Thank you for always telling me that I was going to be somebody and how proud of me you were. Thank you for loving me unconditionally.

To my mom, Rovetta. You have done what no one else in the world could have done. You gave me life. Without you, there would be no me and for that, I thank you. Thank you for seeing it through. Thank you for not throwing me away. Thank you for all you endured. I love you.

To big brother, Tiwan. Thank you for always looking out for me. Thank you for teaching me how to protect myself. You were a horrible big brother (just joking)! But I wouldn't trade you for the world. I love you Big Bro.

To my big sister, Hilda. I admire you so much, and always have. You have always been so strong. I don't know a stronger woman than you. Thank you for showing me what strength looks like. You are truly amazing! I love you.

To Bishop Vernon Kemp, my Pastor. When I came to Greater Harvest, I was in a dark place. Your love, guidance, encouragement, teaching, prayers, and even your correction have my heart overflowing with love for you. I remember when I said I didn't have a dad; you told me you would be my dad. You kept your word, loving and embracing me as your own. You are truly a treasure in my life, and I will always honor you and love you for who you are to me.

To Lady Vicki Kemp. Thank you for your love, leadership, mentorship, and example of grace, class, and character. Your heart for women is phenomenal! Thank you for just being you. Thank you for every conversation, lesson, and prayer for me. Thank you for being a true friend. I love you.

To Mother Cora Jordan. Thank you for taking me in and embracing me as your own. Thank you for every word of wisdom you have shared with me. Thank you for being open and transparent with me and allowing me to come for direction. Thank you for always encouraging me to live holy. Thank you for being wise counsel to me. I thank you for the life you live. I value every opportunity I get to spend time with you. I love you.

To Prophetess Bridgett Barnes. You sparked something in me! Thank you for pouring into me. Thank you for freely giving of yourself. Thank you for challenging me. Thank you for speaking into my life. Thank you for praying for me. I love you.

A special thanks to Vicki Kemp Book Coaching and Consulting and Christian Living Books, Inc. whose dedication and expertise have transformed my manuscript into a polished book. Your meticulous attention to detail and constructive feedback have been crucial in refining and enhancing the final product. Thank you for bringing my words to life.

To all of my GHCC family! I love you. Deacon Jerry and Mrs. Adriane Scott, thank you for your wisdom and guidance and for adopting me as your own. I love you for real! My Finance Family, thank you from the bottom of my heart. I love you, too.

To Mrs. Caroline Barraza, my 6th grade teacher. You saw me then, and you see me now. I will never forget your kindness towards me, your words of encouragement to me, and the faith you had in me. You were a difference-maker in my life.

I am profoundly grateful to the individuals who have shared their personal stories with me over the years. Your openness and vulnerability empowered me to open up. Your courage in overcoming your own challenges has been an inspiration.

Lastly, I would like to acknowledge the broader community of readers and advocates who continually seek to understand and address the complexities of overcoming challenges. Your passion for personal growth and resilience is a reminder of why this work matters.

Thank you all for being a part of this journey. Your contributions, support, and belief have made this book possible and I am forever grateful.

About the Author

Evangelist Maxine Henry, born on September 17, 1977, in Los Angeles, CA, is the youngest of three children to Harold and Rovetta Johnson. For nearly a decade, she has been happily married to her husband and best friend, Elder Roger Henry, Jr. Together, they have six children and eight "Mini Mees." Professionally, Evangelist Henry holds a Bachelor of Science degree in Industrial Psychology and works as a Pension Plan Administrator for a local CPA firm, applying her expertise in the field of accounting.

At Greater Harvest Christian Center Bakersfield, under the leadership of Bishop Vernon R. Kemp and Lady Vicki L. Kemp, Evangelist Henry serves in multiple capacities. She is a dedicated Sunday School teacher for both youth and women's classes, sharing her knowledge and faith with diverse groups. Her commitment to the church's financial well-being led her from volunteering on the financial team to being promoted to the position of church financial controller after three years of faithful service. In 2016, recognizing her spiritual gifts and dedication, she received her evangelist license under the same leadership.

Despite her busy schedule, Evangelist Henry cherishes time spent with her family. She also has a passion for traveling and indulging in fine dining experiences. Reading serves as her favorite pastime, offering moments of relaxation and learning, while writing provides a personal getaway, allowing her to express her thoughts and experiences. Through all aspects of her life, Evangelist Henry finds guidance and inspiration in her favorite scripture, Jude 24: "Now unto Him who is able to keep you from falling, and to present you faultless before the presence of His glory with exceeding joy."

Connect with Maxine

- Maxine Henry
- Maxine_Henry
- @calledchosensent
- _MaxineHenry
- youshallovercome.com
- yesyoushallovercome@gmail.com

www.ingramcontent.com/pod-product-compliance
Lightning Source LLC
Chambersburg PA
CBHW040251170426
43191CB00018B/2375